Weight Loss Secrets For Women Over 50

3 Books in 1 - Keto Diet, Intermittent Fasting & Instant Pot Cookbook: Kick-Start Your Metabolism and Look and Feel Great!

Would you like immediate access to a FREE BOOK? kick start your weight loss journey by transforming your body into a 24/7 fat burning machine!

Ketogenic Diet 101 → Click here to access or go to https://books4u2345-0708f.gr8.com/

Table of Contents

BOOK 1: INTERMITTENT FASTING FOR WOMEN OVER 50	**7**
INTRODUCTION	10
CHAPTER 1 INTERMITTENT FASTING 101	13
WHAT IS IT?	13
HOW DOES IT WORK?	13
WHAT ARE THE ADVANTAGES?	15
WHAT ARE THE DISADVANTAGES?	18
CHAPTER 2 INTERMITTENT FASTING AND WOMEN	21
WOMEN AND FASTING	21
SO WHAT SHOULD WOMEN DO ABOUT FASTING?	21
WHEN INTERMITTENT FASTING IS RISKIER FOR WOMEN	23
CHAPTER 3 IDEAL INTERMITTENT FASTING PROTOCOLS FOR WOMEN	25
THE 12-HOUR FAST	25
LEANGAINS	26
EAT STOP EAT	27
THE WARRIOR DIET	28
FAT LOSS FOREVER	30
ALTERNATE DAY FASTING	31
INTERMITTENT FASTING PLANS AT A GLANCE	32
CHAPTER 4 INTERMITTENT FASTING ACTION PLAN	33
CHAPTER 5 THE COMBINATION THAT TRULY WORKS	37
CHAPTER 6 MUST KNOW INTERMITTENT FASTING GUIDELINES	41
CHAPTER 7 WOMEN AND INTERMITTENT FASTING EXTENDED DISCUSSION	47
CHAPTER 8 INTERMITTENT FASTING 7-DAY PLAN & PROGRESS CHART	48
CHAPTER 9 BREAKFAST RECIPES	50
CHAPTER 10 MAIN MEALS	63
CHAPTER 11 DESERTS	69
CONCLUSION	82
BOOK 2: KETO FOR WOMEN OVER 50	**84**
INTRODUCTION	83
CHAPTER ONE: WHAT IS THE KETOGENIC DIET?	84
THE STATE OF KETOSIS	84
CHAPTER TWO: WHY GO KETO?	86
CHAPTER 3 BREAKFAST RECIPES	90

Sweet Blueberry Pancakes	90
Keto Style Bacon & Eggs	92
Eggs Baked in Avocados	96
Chapter 4 Lunch Recipes	**97**
Chicken Sandwich	97
Meatballs with Bacon and Cheese	99
Steak Salad	101
Almond Pizza	103
Chapter 5 Dinner Recipes	**105**
Shrimp & Bacon Chowder	105
Creamy Salmon	107
Orange Chicken	109
Duck with Sauce	111
Pan-Seared Steak	113
Chapter 6 Vegetarian Recipes	**115**
Spinach Soup	115
Asparagus Frittata	117
Bell Peppers Soup	119
Radish Hash Browns	121
Chapter 7 Vegan Recipes	**122**
Celery Soup	122
Spring Greens Soup	124
Alfalfa Sprouts Salad	126
Eggplant Stew	127
Chapter 8 Desserts (NEW Bonus Chapter!)	**129**
Almond Cookies	129
Pumpkin Pie Cupcakes	131
Brownies	133
Ice Cream	135
Chapter 9 Snack Recipes (NEW Bonus Chapter!)	**137**
Parmesan Crackers	137
Deviled Eggs	139
Almond Garlic Crackers	141
Fat Bombs	143
Chapter 10 - 21 Day Meal Plan (NEW Bonus Chapter!)	**145**
Conclusion	**149**
BOOK 3: AN INSTANT POT WILL SAVE YOUR LIFE…!	**150**
Introduction	151
Chapter One: Breakfast Recipes	155

SPANISH EGGS	155
COCONUT PORRIDGE	157
CHOC-BANANA BREAD	160
BANANA NUT OATMEAL	162
TASTY MORNING PANCAKES	164
EGG BITES	166
CHAPTER TWO: LUNCH RECIPES	**168**
INSTANT POT BARBECUE RIBS	168
SPAGHETTI AND MEATBALLS	170
CHICKEN WITH GRAVY	172
MAC AND CHEESE	174
SPANISH RICE	176
HAWAIIAN CHICKEN	178
CHAPTER THREE: DINNER RECIPES	**180**
CHICKEN ENCHILADA CASSEROLE	180
SHREDDED CHICKEN SALSA	182
CHICKEN BURRITO LASAGNA	184
BUFFALO CHICKEN LETTUCE WRAPS	186
MASHED RANCH CAULIFLOWER	188
LIME CHICKEN TACOS	190
BONUS CHAPTER: CHOCOLATE DESSERTS	**192**
NUTELLA LAVA CAKES	192
CHOCOLATE POTS DE CRÈME	195
CONCLUSION	**197**

©Copyright 2020 by Karen Corcoran All rights reserved.

This document is geared towards providing exact and reliable information in regards to the topic and issue covered. The publication is sold with the idea that the publisher is not required to render accounting, officially permitted, or otherwise, qualified services. If advice is necessary, legal or professional, a practiced individual in the profession should be ordered.

- From a Declaration of Principles which was accepted and approved equally by a Committee of the American Bar Association and a Committee of Publishers and Associations.

In no way is it legal to reproduce, duplicate, or transmit any part of this document in either electronic means or in printed format. Recording of this publication is strictly prohibited and any storage of this document is not allowed unless with written permission from the publisher. All rights reserved.

The information provided herein is stated to be truthful and consistent, in that any liability, in terms of inattention or otherwise, by any usage or abuse of any policies, processes, or directions contained within is the solitary and utter responsibility of the recipient reader. Under no circumstances will any legal responsibility or blame be held against the publisher for any reparation, damages, or monetary loss due to the information herein, either directly or indirectly.

Respective authors own all copyrights not held by the publisher.

The information herein is offered for informational purposes solely, and is universal as so. The presentation of the information is without contract or any type of guarantee assurance.

The trademarks that are used are without any consent, and the publication of the trademark is without permission or backing by the trademark owner. All trademarks and brands within this book are for clarifying purposes only and are the owned by the owners themselves, not affiliated with this document.

It is not legal to reproduce, duplicate, or transmit any part of this document in either electronic means or in printed format. Recording of this publication is strictly prohibited and any storage of this document is not allowed unless with written permission from the publisher except for the use of brief quotations in a book review.

Book 1: Intermittent Fasting for Women Over 50

A Complete Guide to Instant Weight Loss and Healthy Living

By Karen Corcoran
2nd Edition

Would you like immediate access to a FREE BOOK? kick start your weight loss journey by transforming your body into a 24/7 fat burning machine!

Ketogenic Diet 101 → Click here to access or go to https://books4u2345-0708f.gr8.com/

Introduction

I want to personally thank you and congratulate you for purchasing the book *"Intermittent Fasting for Women Over 50: A Complete Guide to Instant Weight Loss and Healthy Living"*.

Losing weight is desirable to us. This is the reason people follow different diets to lose weight and get in shape. However, often we forgot the ancient secret that helped humans to survive throughout the evolution and can help us today to lose weight and lead a healthy life – intermittent fasting.

Are you looking for a proven strategy that will not only help you lose weight but also improve your health? If you answered yes, this guide on intermittent fasting for women is for you. Science proves that intermittent fasting is an effective way for women to lose weight and live happier and healthier lives. Intermittent fasting is very different than starving. If you can follow it in a planned way, this eating pattern can produce amazing health and weight loss benefits. If you are tired of food restrictions, calorie counting, obsessing about food all day, or eliminating foods from your diet, then intermittent fasting is for you. The benefits of intermittent fasting don't stop at weight loss.

Intermittent fasting can help you:

- lower your blood pressure;
- lower your risk of heart disease;
- lower your risk of developing diabetes;
- halt the aging process;
- boost energy;
- balance your hormones; and
- improve your overall well-being.

Have you tried various diets and tricks to lose weight without long lasting success? Forget those and give this proven method a go. This guide is a detailed and informative guide to everything that intermittent fasting has to offer. If you are ready to take control of your health and avoid unnecessary complications, then you need this comprehensive intermittent fasting guide.

Thanks again for purchasing this book, I hope you enjoy it!

Please leave a review!

A lot of research and work goes into our books to make the content the best quality for you – our customers. Therefore, we would love it if you left us a review on Amazon! Please go to:

http://www.amazon.com/review/create-review?&asin=B087QR2Z9H

Any comments would be greatly appreciated. We take all comments very seriously and use these comments to update the content and quality of our books for you and the other readers.

Chapter 1 Intermittent Fasting 101

What is it?

Intermittent fasting has been one of the hottest health trends over the past few years. It refers to refraining from eating for a fixed amount of time during the period when you usually consume calories.

How does it work?

Intermittent fasting is a simple process. Usually, we eat throughout the day. When we wake up, we eat breakfast, then lunch, usually a snack in the afternoon followed by dinner. If you are eating your breakfast at 7 a.m., and dinner at 8 p.m., then these 13 hours are your "eating window." What intermittent fasting does is shorten this eating window. Most beginners can start with a 16-hour fast which means following an 8-hour eating window. For example, you eat your dinner at 8 p.m. then skip breakfast the next morning and eat your lunch at 12 p.m. So you perform a 16-hour fast without any difficulty. You are basically skipping only breakfast. At first, it might feel uneasy for you, but after a few days of fasting, you will get accustomed to the intermittent fasting. Although the intermittent fasting has become popular in recent years, it is not new. Humans have been fasting since ancient times. For example, our Paleolithic ancestors use to fast when food was unavailable.

Starvation and Fasting

Starvation is when you are forced to fast. It has no fixed time limit. Beginners often misunderstood intermittent fasting with starvation. Starvation is a situation where you are forced to fast because you have no access to food. On the other hand, when following intermittent fasting, you have access to food but delay eating it for a few hours to one or two days. During intermittent fasting, you are in control of the situation and can break your fast if you feel uneasy. But with starvation, you do not have a choice. You are not forced to fast. Starvation has no fixed time frame.

You can start with a 16-hour fast. See how you feel and then extend the time to a day (24-hours). Fasting is actually a part of modern life. We eat "breakfast" daily. This break-fast simply means that we were fasting during the night and need to eat in the morning to break the fast. So indirectly, the term "breakfast" is actually signaling to us that we already fast daily. You just need to extend the time duration for the fast to become effective.

In the early phases of human evolution, humans weren't eating three meals daily with a few snacks in between. Our hunter-gatherer ancestors didn't have an abundance of access to food as you and I do today. They had to hunt or collect food from the wild to eat. Because of this process, they sometimes went without food for days. They ate when they gathered food and then had to fast when the food was scarce.

What are the Advantages?

The are many advantages of intermittent fasting. These include by are not limited to the following.

1. *Intermittent fasting changes the function of cells, genes, and hormones for the better.*

   Studies show that intermittent fasting triggers cellular repair processes and alters hormone levels, so your body's stored fat deposits are more accessible. When you fast, your insulin levels drop, and the production of human growth hormones increases. If your insulin levels drop your body can burn stored body fat. Increased human growth hormones help with body repairs (US National Library of Medicine).

Fat Burning During Fasting

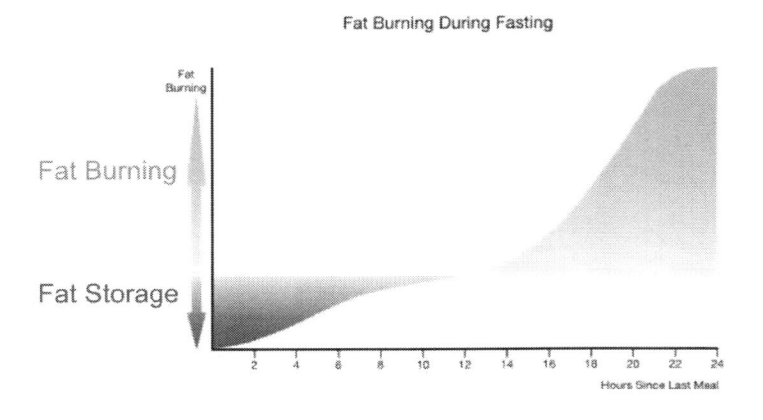

2. *Intermittent fasting helps you to lose weight.*

   Intermittent fasting boosts hormone functions that trigger weight loss. It produces a higher growth in hormone levels, lower insulin levels, and increased amounts of norepinephrine which all increase the breakdown of body fat and also boost your metabolic rate (US National Library of Medicine).

3. *Lowers your risk of type 2 diabetes.*

   Diabetes has become a deadly disease in recent years. Following an intermittent fasting plan can help you regulate your insulin levels and lower your risk of getting type 2 diabetes (Science Direct).

4. *Reduce oxidative stress and inflammation in the body.*

   It is the oxidative stress that triggers all sorts of chronic diseases in the body. Intermittent fasting enhances the body's ability to fight oxidative stress. Additionally, studies show that intermittent fasting can lower inflammation in the body.

5. *Beneficial for heart health (US National Library of Medicine).*

   Currently, heart disease is the world's biggest killer. Risk factors of heart disease include high blood sugar levels, inflammatory markers, blood triglycerides, total and LDL cholesterol, and high blood pressure. Intermittent fasting can lower all of these risk factors, improve heart health, and lower the risk of heart disease (IBIMA Publishing).

6. *Induces various cellular repair processes.*

   When practiced daily, Intermittent fasting triggers autophagy. During autophagy, our bodies recycle damaged proteins, remove harmful and toxic compounds. Increased autophagy protects the human body from various diseases, including Alzheimer's and various types of cancers (US National Library of Medicine).

7. *Good for brain function.*

   Intermittent fasting improves various metabolic features that are crucial for brain health. This includes reduced inflammation, reduced oxidative stress, and a reduction in blood sugar levels and insulin resistance. A reduction of all of these benefits the health and functioning of your brain (Wiley Online Library).

What are the Disadvantages?

There are some side effects of fasting. These may include the following.

1. *Dehydration*

   Beginner dieters who start to fast often feel dehydrated at times. However, intermittent fasting only asks you to avoid calorie-rich foods and drinks. So drink plenty of water during your fast to avoid dehydration.

2. *Stress*

People who never fasted before will feel stress when they start to fast. You are used to eating breakfast, lunch, and dinner. Now suddenly you have to avoid eating breakfast or lunch or both. So you might feel a bit anxious and stressed. It is normal, and do not worry! You will not die if you avoid eating 1 or 2 meals daily. Humans have been fasting since Paleolithic times. If fasting was a life-threatening event, then humans would have become extinct a long time ago. Additionally, you can break your fast anytime that you feel uneasy. This is not a mandatory event. If you feel too much stress as you adjust into a fasting pattern, you can break your fast and eat something if you feel this is necessary.

3. *Heartburn*

Not eating food for a long time can lower stomach acid. However, thinking about food or smelling food can trigger acid production and cause heartburn. If you notice that you are continuously thinking about food or roaming around in the kitchen or circling around food items continuously, then you are not yet ready for the long term fast. So eat something and break your fast. Practice shorter fasts such as an 8-hour fast first, then when your body is ready, you can move to a 12-hour fast.

4. *People with underlying illnesses*

IMPORTANT NOTE: People who are already sick with a disease such as heart disease, diabetes, or cancer patients should check with their doctor or health care professional before they start fasting to avoid any complications or further health risks.

Chapter 2 Intermittent Fasting and Women

Women and Fasting

The impact that intermittent fasting has on women is a little different to that of men. The female reproductive system and metabolism are deeply entwined. Usually, women consume less protein than men, and fasting women will usually consume even less. Consuming less protein results in fewer amino acids in the female body. Amino acids are required to stimulate estrogen receptors and synthesize IGF -1 (insulin-like growth factor in the liver).

IGF -1 assist in the progression of the reproductive cycle. So a diet low in protein can lower fertility and sex drive in women. Furthermore, for women, estrogen isn't only needed for reproduction. Women have estrogen receptors throughout their bodies, including bones and brains. Change in estrogen balance in a woman's body can disrupt metabolic function and result in indigestion problems, mood swings, sluggish bone formation, etc.

So what should women do about fasting?

Now you know that a prolonged period of no food is a significant stressor for a woman's body and affects their reproductive health. The good news for you is that the intermittent fasting protocols vary, some more extreme than others (up to 36 hours), which also proves difficult and challenging for healthy males. When fasting, the length of your fast, your age, nutritional status, exercise, and other stresses in your life are all relevant.

If you want to do intermittent fasting, then follow a conservative approach. For example, start your fasting after dinner and don't eat for 12 -14 hours. So you will fast from dinner to lunch the next day. With this method, you are basically skipping only one meal – breakfast. Repeat the procedure every alternate day. So 12-14 hours fast followed by a 1-day break and then fast for 12-14 hours again. Obviously, sleeping time will make fasting easier for you. Don't practice any hard workouts during your fasting day and limit yourself to practicing yoga or low intensity exercise. Follow a routine that makes sense, suits you, and one that you can actually maintain. If needed, start with fasting 2 days a week.

Stop Intermittent Fasting if:

- You notice mood swings

- You always seem to feel cold

- Your digestion slows down noticeably

- You start to develop acne or dry skin

- You have problems falling asleep or staying asleep

- Your menstrual cycle stops or suddenly becomes irregular
- Your heart rate becomes abnormal
- You feel a decline in sex drive
- Your hair falls out
- Your stress tolerance declines
- You recover slowly from injury

Avoid fasting if:

- You have not consulted with a health care professional
- You have a history of eating disorders
- You don't sleep well
- You are chronically stressed
- You are pregnant

When intermittent fasting is riskier for women

If women fast for too long, for example 3-days, then it can be riskier for them. The solution is simple. Do not fast for 3 days straight. A lot of healthy men, such as bodybuilders and athletes, will feel various side effects after fasting for 3 days straight. Stay safe and practice safe fasts such as 8-hour fasts, 12-hour fasts, or 1 day fasts. If you practice a 72-hour fast, then it is normal to experience a few side effects. <u>All women should consult with their doctor before fasting.</u> Especially if any of the following apply to you.

1. Trying to conceive, pregnant or breastfeeding.
2. Have a history of amenorrhea or fertility problems.
3. Are malnourished, underweight, or have nutritional deficiencies
4. Have low blood sugar levels or diabetes.
5. A history of eating disorders.

Chapter 3 Ideal Intermittent Fasting Protocols for Women

Figure 1: Intermittent fasting variants

Image Source: examine.com

The best intermittent fasting protocols for women are as follows.

The 12-hour fast

This fasting plan is easy. You eat breakfast at 7 a.m. Skip lunch and eat dinner at 7 p.m. This plan is very easy and simple for beginners.

Pros

- Easy for the beginners

Cons

- Fasting for only 12-hours doesn't burn too much fat.

Leangains

This fasting method was popularized by Martin Berkhan. Who is also called Khan. He is considered as the high priest or godfather of intermittent fasting. He is a writer, personal trainer and a nutritional consultant. This method requires a 16 hour fast for men and a 14 hour fast for women. Fasters are to feed during the remaining hours. During this fasting period, you consume no calories. However, you are permitted to consume water, black coffee and tea. Starting the fast after dinner, skipping breakfast, and breaking the fast at lunchtime the next day is a popular routine. What you eat and when you eat depends on if and when you exercise. During your exercise days, eating more carbs is recommended. Your fat intake should be higher on your fast days, and protein consumption should remain fairly high every day. However, it all depends on your fast goals, age, activity levels, and body fat.

Pros

- You have an 8-hour eating window to eat whatever you want. This longer eating window gives you the advantage of eating several meals.

Cons

- This fasting protocol has specific guidelines for what to eat, especially if you exercise. This strict scheduling and nutrition plan around exercise can make the plan tougher for some to follow.

Eat Stop Eat

Brad Pilon invented this fasting protocol. He is a fasting enthusiast and one of the world's leading supporters of intermittent fasting. With this method, you fast for a full 24 hours once or twice every week. The inventor Brad Pilon refers to this system as a "24 break from eating". You can't consume any food during your fast, but you are allowed to drink calorie-free beverages. Once your fast is over, you can start to eat normally. Some like to eat a light snack after the fast; others like to break the fast with a big meal. According to Eat Stop Eat, this way of eating will lower your overall calorie consumption without limiting what you are able to eat. The protocol focuses on how often you eat. If improved body composition or weight loss is your goal, then you will need to exercise, especially resistance training, while you fast.

Pros

- This fasting program is flexible, even though 24 hours may seem a long time to fast. You do not have to start with this method. You can practice the easier 14-hour fast until you and your body are adjusted to fasting protocol and then start a 24-hour fast. Also remember, if you feel uneasy during your 24-hour fast, you can break it any time and eat something. Pilon recommends you choose a busy day to fast when you have no eating compulsions such as a family dinner or work lunches.

Cons

- As a beginner, it might be hard for you to start with a 24-hour fast. This might also trigger binge eating when you break your fast.

The Warrior Diet

Ori Hofmekler is the inventor of this fasting protocol. He is an expert on survival science and a supporter of intermittent fasting. With this protocol, you fast for about 20 hours daily and then eat a big meal at night. The Warrior Diet shadows the Paleolithic lifestyle of our ancestors. During the Paleolithic era, our ancestors hunted and gathered food during the day and ate at night. Ori Hofmekler believes that humans are nocturnal eaters, so his fasting protocol goes well with the circadian rhythms of humans. During the 20-hour fast, you can eat a few portions of raw fruit or vegetables. You can also eat a few servings of protein if desired.

This occasional snacking is to maximize the human "fight or flight" response, which is intended to boost energy, promote alertness, and stimulate fat burning. According to Hofmekler, the four-hour eating window is in the night to stimulate the Parasympathetic Nervous System's ability to assist the body to digest, recuperate, relax, and stay calm. Additionally, foods consumed during this time helps the body to burn fat and produce hormones during the day. What you eat during this time also matters. Hofmelker recommends eating protein, fat, and veggies. Then if you feel hungry, eat some carbohydrates.

Pros

- Many like this method because while you fast, you can also consume a few snacks, which make it easier for beginners. Many supporters say they lost fat and felt an increase in energy levels.

Cons

- The guidelines for what to eat and when can be hard for beginners. The strict meal planning and scheduling may also interfere with social gatherings.

Fat Loss Forever

This fasting plan is introduced by John Romaniello and Dan Go. These two men are both are fitness experts and developed an intermittent fasting strategy that guarantees fat loss. If you are not satisfied with any of the above fasting plans, then you might like this one. This plan takes the best parts of The Warrior Diet, Eat Stop Eat, and Leangains and combines it all into one plan. With this plan, you get one cheat day each week. The cheat day is followed by a 36-hour fast. The inventors of this method recommend fasting for 36 hours when they are busy with work. This fasting program also includes an exercise training program to maximize fat loss.

Pros

- The method offers a structured, fast plan which is beneficial.

Cons

- This plan varies from day to day and can be a bit confusing to follow.

Alternate Day Fasting

This fasting plan is introduced by James Johnson, M.D. He is a former assistant professor of otolaryngology. He has done many studies and developed this fasting protocol. This method recommends that you eat around 400 to 500 calories one day and eat normally the next day. Johnson suggests drinking meal replacement shakes during the fast days when you are starting as a beginner. After two weeks you should start eating real foods during your fast days. Eat normally the next day and repeat.

Pros

- This method targets weight loss. So if you want to lose weight, then this plan will be good for you.

Cons

You need to plan your meals for your non-fast days. Otherwise, this plan won't work.

Intermittent fasting plans at a glance

12-hour fast	You fast for 12 hours with this method.
Leangains	This plan recommends 16-hour fast for men, and 14-hour fast for women.
Eat Stop Eat	This plan calls for a full 24-hour fast once or twice every week.
The Warrior Diet	You have to fast for 20 hours daily with this plan.
Fat Loss Forever	This plan calls for 36-hour fast
Alternate Day Fasting	With this plan, you fast one day and then eat normally the next day.

Chapter 4 Intermittent Fasting Action Plan

A week of preparation is a great way to start transitioning yourself into intermittent fasting. The following is a seven-day plan that we recommend you start prior to your first fast.

Day 1: Motivate yourself

Compile your favorite motivational quotes in a notepad or into a document on your laptop. Print and cut them out and place them in easily viewable location in your house. It might include your kitchen, your bathroom or your work desk. Take the time to read and reflect on them throughout the week. Believe it or not but this actually works!

Day 2: Stay focused

When you are trying to reach a goal, visualization is the best method. Make two vision boards, one for work, and one for your home. You can use a sheet of cardboard or a simple bulletin board for this. Collect pictures that inspire, perhaps, pictures of the past when you were fit and healthy and looked attractive. You may want to combine these pictures with your motivational quotes.

Day 3: The Beginning and the destination

Know your starting position, so you will know where you will arrive. The first thing you need to do is take your measurements. Take your measurements one day prior to your fast. Use a flexible tape measure, measure your calves, thighs, hips, abdomen, waist, upper arms, and chest. Record the measurements every 1-2 weeks and compare them. This will allow you to keep track of your weight loss progress. Use an online body mass index calculator (BMI calculator). Calculate your BMI once every 1 to 2 weeks after starting intermittent fasting.

Day 4: Set your goals

Write down the goals that you want to achieve with intermittent fasting. Here are some pointers:

- I will fast for 16 hours for 3 days of the week/ I will fast for 2 (24-hour each) days of the week/ I will fast for 36 hours.

- I will drink a minimum of 64 ounces of water daily.

- I will swim 25 laps twice every week.

- I will walk to work three times every week. I will try to lose at least 4 pounds each month until I reach my desired weigh loss goal.

- I will do at least 30 minutes of moderate exercise every week.

Place your goals in a spot that you frequently roam, such as in front of the freezer. Change your goals every couple of weeks to keep yourself excited and moving forward.

Day 5: Make a reward program for yourself

For every goal you reach, write down a list of rewards you will enjoy. Rewards can be as simple as spending 20 minutes on Facebook, buying your favorite magazine, or a night out with your friends.

Day 6: Fast for 12-hours

Day 6, you start your fasting program. You never fasted before, so start with a 12-hour fast. It is easy, eat your breakfast, then skip lunch and eat dinner. This will enable you to observe a 12-hour fast.

Day 7: Notice how you feel

On Day 7, notice how you are feeling in the morning. Are you feeling well? Are you able to skip breakfast and able to fast for 16 hours? You can skip breakfast and see what happens. Drink water and keep yourself busy with work. If you feel unwell, then break your fast and eat lunch. Otherwise, wait for 14-hour to complete your fast.

Chapter 5 The Combination that Truly Works

There are benefits to combining intermittent fasting and the keto diet. The ketogenic diet has gained popularity during the last few years because it has helped people to lose weight while establishing many health benefits. When you follow a keto diet, it pushes your body into a state known as ketosis. In ketosis, the body creates a different fuel source (ketones) to provide energy for the body. Your body uses glucose as a primary source of energy with a carb-rich diet. With a low-carb diet, your body uses fat as the main source of energy.

The keto diet has the following benefits.

1. *Decreases your appetite*

    Eating a keto diet lowers your appetite. This is because fat has a very filling effect which helps to decrease appetite. Additionally, you can drink water and curb hunger. So practicing a 14-hour fast will soon become easy for you.

2. *Weight loss*

    With keto, you are eating less carbs. And with intermittent fasting you avoiding eating for a certain amount of time. Both jointly help you to lose weight.

3. *Reach ketosis faster*

By following the keto diet, you restrict carbs, so your body starts to burn fat for energy. Additionally, you are fasting at the same time, which causes your body's glycogen levels to drop. This combination fast-tracks your body to ketosis. Also, this combination can help you avoid keto flu. Keto flu is a flu type symptom you may temporarily experience when you first start the diet.

4. *Triggers autophagy*

In 2016, Yoshinori Ohsumi won a Nobel Prize for discovering some crucial aspects of autophagy. During autophagy, our bodies recycle damaged proteins, remove harmful and toxic compounds, and boost the production of ketones quicker than on the standard Ketogenic diet. This process is important for reversing diabetes, preventing cancer, and stopping the aging process. However, autophagy only occurs when you restrict carb, protein consumption, and fast. All three happen when you combine the keto diet with intermittent fasting.

5. Helps stabilize blood sugar levels

If you eat carb-rich foods and practice intermittent fasting, your body is constantly switching between glucose and ketones for energy. This can cause a spike in blood sugar levels, mood swings, brain fog, low energy, and other side effects. Combining keto and intermittent fasting restricts carb consumption and eliminates unhealthy blood sugar spikes and other side effects.

If you would like to learn more about the keto diet, you can download the following book for FREE!

Ketogenic Diet 101

CLICK HERE to access.

Keto For Women Over 50

Alternatively, we have another book on amazon titled "Keto For Women Over 50: Simple 30 Minute Recipes for Instant Weight Loss and Healthy Living"

CLICK HERE to access.

Chapter 6 Must Know Intermittent Fasting Guidelines

Must follow guidelines

1. *Chart your progress*

    Make a plan and write it down. Keeping a diary is useful to see if this diet is working for you. Data shows that dieters who write daily notes are more successful at losing weight with intermittent fasting.

2. *Prep*

    Prep your fast-day food in advance. This will help you to maintain the keto diet and intermittent fasting combination.

3. *Breaking your fast*

    Break your fast with a snack. Often we overeat as soon as the fast is over. We eat more because of a psychological need. Not because of hunger. When your fast is over, eat a small snack or a small dish, then wait for 30 minutes to an hour then eat your main meal. This will help you to avoid overeating. Here are some suggestions for your first snack when you break your fast:
    - A small bowl of soup
    - A small amount of meat
    - A small bowl of raw vegetables
    - A small salad

- 1/3 cup nuts

4. *Avoid suppressing*

    Don't try to suppress your thoughts of food during your fast. It is because of a psychological mechanism called habituation. If you have something in abundance, then you put less value on it. So trying to suppress the thought of food during your fast is the wrong strategy. Do not try to associate fasting with discomfort.

5. Stay hydrated
6. Drink plenty of water. Remember, a dry mouth is a sign of dehydration, so act before your body complains. Drink approximately 8 big glasses of water. Drinking water will help you to suppress your hunger.

7. *Weight loss*

    How much weight you will lose depends on your body type, your activity level, your starting weight, your metabolism, and how much you consume during your non-fast days.
    If not losing weight:
    - Be patient. Some people need a longer time to lose weight.
    - Be realistic. The average weight loss is more likely to be around 1 to 2 pounds per week.
    - Avoid binging.
    - Keep a food diary.
    - Look at the calories you are receiving from fizzy drinks, smoothies, alcohol, juices, lattes, and drinks.
    - Try adding more fast days

8. *Breakfast is vital?*

   Often, people say that breakfast is vital. However, a study concluded that both breakfast eaters and skippers lost the same amount of weight.

9. *Drinks during no fast days*

   Drink lots of water. Use lemon, mint leaves, cloves, ginger, and lemongrass to flavor your water. Drink herbal teas such as lavender, chamomile, rose, ginger, cinnamon, lemongrass, and licorice.

10. *Supplements*

    You do not need any supplements, but if you are fond of supplements, then here are a few that you can take during your fast days:
    - Glucosamine – ideal for relieving joint pain.
    - Casein Protein – ideal for pre-bedtime.
    - Whey Protein – Protein boost for pre and post-workout.
    - Beta-Alanine – boosts exercise performance.
    - Branched Chain Amino Acids (BCAA) – can help limit lean body mass loss as well as increasing visceral fat loss.
    - Vitamin D – helps you function optimally.
    - Calcium – increases fast excretion and boosts testosterone.
    - Fish oil – helps keep your Omega – 3 and 6 levels up.

- Multivitamin – to overcome any deficiencies you may have.

11. Gender differences

Men and women have metabolic and hormonal differences. They store and utilize fat in different ways. Fasting aids both sexes, and studies show positive results. However, fasting is not meant to be a struggle, so be cautious and self-aware. Listen to your body.

12. *Fasting during menstruation*

Some women may find fasting more challenging in the days preceding a period. If you feel any discomfort, then avoid fasting during your period.

13. *When trying to conceive*

The science is still unfolding, but health experts say an intermittent fasting plan will not affect fertility. But more extreme fasting may (such as 36-hour fast). Be cautious and avoid fasting when you are trying to get pregnant.

14. *If you have headaches*
Headaches occur due to dehydration rather than fasting itself. Drink plenty of water during your fast.

15. *Constipation*
It can happen if you have too fiber in your diet.

16. *Affecting sleep*

Some people find it difficult to go to bed hungry. Drink a glass of milk or eat a small snack before bed.

17. *Time-frame*

    Do not fast for more than 36 hours. Fasting for a long time will trigger various negative symptoms, which you want to avoid. If you fast for too long, you will start to lose muscle and protein tissue instead of fat. You want to lose fat to lose weight. Losing too much muscle will make you unhealthy.

18. *Do not rush*

    If you have a certain health condition, then do not rush into fasting. Discuss with your doctor before starting intermittent fasting.

Health concerns

1. *Muscle cramps*

    Low magnesium can cause muscle cramps. Take an over-the-counter magnesium supplement, or you can apply magnesium oil on your skin.

2. *Heartburn*

    Do not eat a large meal when you break your fast. It might cause heartburn. Drinking sparkling water with lemon often helps.

3. *Constipation*

    Increase your intake of fiber, vegetables, and fruits during your non-fasting days to prevent constipation.

4. *Dizziness*

    Consume regular levels of salt and water daily to cure dizziness. Also, low blood pressure may be a cause of dizziness.

Chapter 7 Women and Intermittent Fasting Extended Discussion

Special benefits for women

1. *Anti-aging*
   The autophagy is triggered during fasting. Autophagy breaks down cellular "waste." Rebuilding stronger, more effective cells and tissues for a cleaner, efficient body. This slows down the aging process.

2. *Lower inflammation*
   A lot of women experience inflammation and swelling, either periodically or on a regular basis. During intermittent fasting, inflammation is reduced.

3. *Hormonal balance*
   Intermittent fasting can better regulate hormonal production in the body. This can improve symptoms experienced before and during a menstrual cycle and during other hormonal changes during pre-menopause.

Chapter 8 Intermittent Fasting 7-Day Plan & Progress Chart

Week of...

DAY	START TIME	1ST MEAL	2ND MEAL	3RD MEAL	END TIME
SUNDAY					
MONDAY					
TUESDAY					
WEDNESDAY					
THURSDAY					
FRIDAY					
SATURDAY					

PROGRESS CHART

Date	Weight	L/R Arm	L/R Leg	Chest	Waist	Hip

Chapter 9 Breakfast Recipes

Pancakes

Prep time: 5 minutes | Cook time: 15 minutes | Servings: 4

Ingredients

- Egg – 1, large
- Egg whites – 2
- Cream cheese – 2 tbsp.
- Unsweetened, canned pumpkin – 3 tbsp. (not pie filling)
- Vanilla extract – 1 tbsp.
- Almond flour - 2/3 cup
- Coconut flour – 2 tbsp.
- Swerve sweetener – 1 tbsp.
- Pumpkin pie spice – 1 tsp.
- Salt – 1/8 tsp.
- Baking powder – 1 tsp.
- Baking soda – ¼ tsp.
- Xanthan gum – ½ tsp.
- Water as needed

Topping:

- Cream cheese – 1/3 cup
- Unsweetened canned pumpkin – 2 tbsp.
- Swerve sweetener – 1 to 1 ½ tbsp.
- Cinnamon – ½ tsp.
- Pumpkin pie spice – 1/8 tsp.
- Vanilla extract – ½ tsp.

Method

1. Preheat a griddle to 350F. Except for the water, add all the wet pancake ingredients into a blender and blend. Then add the dry ingredients and blend until smooth.
2. A little at a time, add water until the pancake batter has the right consistency.
3. In the preheated, oiled griddle, pour a small amount of batter.
4. Cook until browned and the edges (almost to the center) are dry, about 3 to 4 minutes.
5. Then flip and cook for 2 to 3 minutes more.
6. For the topping: in a processor, add all topping ingredients and blend until creamy.
7. Top the pancakes with toppings and drizzle with maple syrup.

Nutritional Facts Per Serving (3-inch)

- Calories 230
- Protein 8 g
- Carb 9.5 g
- Fat 16 g

Oatmeal

Prep time: 5 minutes   Cook time: 10 minutes   Servings: 6

Ingredients

- Chia seeds - 1/3 cup
- Crushed pecans - 1 cup
- Cauliflower - 1/2 cup, riced
- Flaxseed meal - 1/3 cup
- Coconut milk - 3 1/2 cups
- Butter - 3 tbsp.
- Heavy cream - 1/4 cup
- Cream cheese - 3 oz.
- Maple flavor - 1 tsp.
- Cinnamon - 1 1/2 tsp.
- Erythritol - 3 tbsp. powdered
- Vanilla - 1/2 tsp.
- Allspice - 1/4 tsp.
- Nutmeg - 1/4 tsp.
- Liquid stevia - 10-15 drops
- Xanthan gum -1/8 tsp. (optional)

Method

1. Heat milk over medium heat in a pan.
2. Crush pecans and add to the pan over low heat to toast.
3. Now add cauliflower to the coconut milk and bring to a boil. Reduce to simmer, add spices and mix.
4. Grind erythritol and add to the pan. Then add chia seeds, flax, stevia and mix well.
5. Add butter, cream, and cream cheese to the pan and mix well.
6. Add xanthan gum to make it a bit thicker.
7. Serve.

Nutritional Facts Per Serving

- Calorie 398
- Fat 37.7g
- Carb 3.1g
- Protein 8.8g

Veggie Omelet

Prep time: 5 minutes   Cook time: 12 minutes   Servings: 1

Ingredients

- Eggs – 3
- Almond milk or water – 1 tbsp.
- Kosher salt – ½ tsp.
- Freshly ground black pepper – ½ tsp.
- Unsalted butter – 3 tbsp.
- Swiss chard – 1 bunch, cleaned and stemmed
- Ricotta – 1/3 cup

Method

1. Crack the eggs in a bowl. Add water or milk, season with salt and pepper. Beat with a fork and set aside.
2. Melt 2 tbsp. the butter over medium-high heat in an 8-inch nonstick skillet.
3. Add a few of the veggie leaves and continue to sauté until just wilted. Remove from pan. Set aside.
4. Now melt 1 tbsp. butter in the skillet.

5. Then slowly add the egg mixture and tilt the pan, so the mixture spreads evenly. Allow the egg to firm up a bit. Cook for another 1 minute.

6. Spoon in the ricotta when the edges are firm, but the center is still a bit runny.

7. With a spatula, fold about 1/3 of the omelet over the ricotta filling.

8. Serve on a plate with Swiss chard.

Nutritional Facts Per Serving

- Calories 693
- Fat 60g
- Carb 8g
- Protein 31g

Ham Omelet

Prep time: 5 minutes   Cook time: 10 minutes   Servings: 5

Ingredients

- Unsalted butter – 1 ½ tbsp.
- Eggs – 10
- Milk – 2 tbsp.
- Kosher salt – 1 tsp.
- Freshly ground black pepper – ¼ tsp.
- Cooked ham – 1 ¼ cups, diced
- Shredded sharp cheddar – 1 ½ cups
- Fresh chives – 1/3 cup, chopped

Method

1. Melt the butter in a skillet. Add ham and sauté until browned.
2. Meanwhile, whisk together the eggs, pepper, kosher salt, and milk in a bowl.
3. Pour into the pan and cook for 4 to 5 minutes, or until the desired doneness. Stirring occasionally.
4. Just before the eggs are set, add chives and cheddar.

Nutritional Facts Per Serving

- Calories 369.36
- Fat 26.74g
- Carb 2.21g
- Protein 28.69g

Salmon with Sauce

Prep time: 5 minutes   Cook time: 15 minutes   Servings: 2

Ingredients

- Salmon fillet - 1 1/2 lb.
- Duck fat - 1 tbsp.
- Dried dill weed - ¾ to 1 tsp.
- Dried tarragon - ¾ to 1 tsp.
- Salt and pepper to taste

Cream Sauce

- Heavy cream - 1/4 cup
- Butter - 2 tbsp.
- Dried dill weed - 1/2 tsp.
- Dried tarragon - 1/2 tsp.
- Salt and pepper to taste

Method

1. Slice the salmon in half and make 2 fillets. Season skin side with salt and pepper and meat of the fish with spices.
2. In a skillet, heat 1 tbsp. duck fat over medium heat.
3. Add salmon to the hot pan, skin side down.

4. Cook the salmon for about 5 minutes. When the skin is crisp, lower the heat and flip salmon.

5. Cook salmon on low heat for 7 to 15 minutes, or until your desired doneness is reached.

6. Remove salmon from the pan and set aside.

7. Add spices and butter in the pan and let brown. Once browned, add cream and mix.

8. Top salmon with sauce and serve.

Nutritional Facts Per Serving

- Calorie 469
- Fat 40g
- Carb 1.5g
- Protein 22.5g

Butter Chicken

Prep time: 5 minutes   Cook time: 30 minutes   Servings: 4

Ingredients

- Butter – ¼ cup
- Mushrooms – 2 cups, sliced
- Chicken thighs – 4 large
- Onion powder – ½ tsp.
- Garlic powder – ½ tsp.
- Kosher salt – 1 tsp.
- Black pepper – ¼ tsp.
- Water – ½ cup
- Dijon mustard – 1 tsp.
- Fresh tarragon – 1 tbsp., chopped

Method

1. Season the chicken thighs with onion powder, garlic powder, salt, and pepper.
2. In a sauté pan, melt 1 tbsp. butter.
3. Sear the chicken thighs about 3 to 4 minutes per side, or until both sides are golden brown. Remove the thighs from the pan.
4. Add the remaining 3 tbsp. of butter to the pan and melt.

5. Add the mushrooms and cook for 4 to 5 minutes, or until golden brown. Stirring as little as possible.

6. Add the Dijon mustard and water to the pan. Stir to deglaze.

7. Place the chicken thighs back to the pan, keep the skin side up.

8. Cover and simmer for 15 minutes.

9. Stir in the fresh herbs, let sit for 5 minutes and serve.

Nutritional Facts Per Serving

- Calories 447
- Fat 31g
- Carb 1g
- Protein 37g

Chapter 10 Main Meals

Chicken Salad

Prep time: 10 minutesCook time: 20 minutesServings: 1

Ingredients

- Chicken breast – 1
- Cherry tomatoes – 3
- Avocado – ½
- Red onion – 1 tbsp.
- Sesame seed oil – 2 tbsp.
- Lettuce – 1, handful
- Mayonnaise – 2 tbsp.
- Paprika – 1 tsp.

Method

1. Cook the chicken breast in the oven for 20 minutes at 375F. Remove and sprinkle with paprika.
2. Cut the salad ingredients and place them on a plate.
3. Cut the chicken into pieces and place on top of the salad.

4. Mix the sesame seed oil and mayonnaise and use as a dressing.
5. Serve.

Nutritional Facts Per Serving

- Calories: 852
- Fat: 45g
- Carb: 5g
- Protein: 65g

Shrimp Stew

Prep time: 10 minutes   Cook time: 15 minutes   Servings: 6

Ingredients

- Onion – ¼ cup, peeled and chopped
- Olive oil – ¼ cup
- Garlic – 1 clove, peeled and minced
- Shrimp – 1 ½ pounds, peeled and deveined
- Red pepper – ¼ cup, roasted and chopped
- Canned diced tomatoes – 14 ounces
- Fresh cilantro – ¼ cup, chopped
- Sriracha sauce – 2 tbsp.
- Coconut milk – 1 cup
- Salt and ground black pepper to taste
- Lime juice – 2 tbsp.

Method

1. Heat a pan with oil over medium heat.
2. Add onion and stir-fry for 4 minutes.

3. Add peppers and garlic. Stir-fry for 4 minutes.
4. Add tomatoes, cilantro, shrimp, and stir-fry until shrimp turns pink.
5. Add coconut milk, and sriracha sauce, stir and bring to a gentle simmer.
6. Add the salt, pepper, lime juice, stir and transfer to bowls.
7. Serve.

Nutritional Facts Per Serving

- Calories: 376
- Fat: 25.1g
- Carb: 2.5g
- Protein: 46.3g

Lamb Curry

Prep time: 10 minutes   Cook time: 4 hours   Servings: 6

Ingredients

- Fresh ginger – 2 tbsp. grated
- Garlic – 2 cloves, peeled and minced
- Cardamom – 2 tsp.
- Onion – 1, peeled and hopped
- Cloves – 6
- Lamb meat – 1 pound, cubed
- Cumin powder – 2 tsp.
- Garam masala – 1 tsp.
- Chili powder – ½ tsp.
- Turmeric – 1 tsp.
- Coriander – 2 tsp.
- Spinach – 1 pound
- Canned diced tomatoes – 14 ounces

Method

1. In a slow cooker, mix lamb with tomatoes, spinach, ginger, garlic, onion, cardamom, cloves, cumin, garam masala, chili, turmeric, and coriander.

2. Stir, cover, and cook on high for 4 hours.

3. Uncover slow cooker, stir the chili, divide into bowls, and serve.

Nutritional Facts Per Serving

- Calories: 186
- Fat: 6.1g
- Carb: 9.1g
- Protein: 24.3g

Chapter 11 Deserts

Chocolate Truffles

Prep time: 10 minutes Cook time: 60 minute Servings: 12

Ingredients

- Ripe Hass avocados – 2, pitted and skinned
- Coconut oil – 2 tbsp.
- Premium cocoa powder – ½ cup
- Granulated sugar substitute – 1 tbsp.
- Sugar free chocolate-flavored syrup – 2 tbsp.
- Heavy whipping cream – 2 tbsp.
- Bourbon – 2 tbsp.
- Chopped pecans – ½ cup

Method

1. Except for the pecans, combine all ingredients in a small blender and process until smooth. Chill for 1 hour.
2. Make 1-inch balls and then roll in the pecans.
3. Chill in the refrigerator.

Nutritional Facts Per Serving (1 truffle)

- Calories 111
- Fat 10g
- Carb 4.5g
- Protein 1.5g

Blueberry Cake

Prep time: 10 minutes   Cook time: 40 minutes   Servings: 4

Ingredients

- Almond flour - 2/3 cup
- Eggs – 5
- Almond milk – 1/3 cup
- Erythritol – ¼ cup
- Vanilla extract – 2 tsp.
- Juice of 2 lemons
- Lemon zest – 1 tsp.
- Baking soda – ½ tsp.
- Pinch of salt
- Fresh blueberries – ½ cup
- Butter – 1 to 2 tbsp. melted

For the frosting:

- Heavy cream – ½ cup
- Juice of 1 lemon

- Erythritol– 1/8 cup

Method

1. Preheat the oven to 350F.

2. In a bowl, add the almond flour, eggs, and almond milk and mix well until smooth.

3. Then add the erythritol, a pinch of salt, baking soda, lemon zest, lemon juice, and vanilla extract. Mix and combine well.

4. Fold in the blueberries.

5. Use the butter to grease the springform pans.

6. Pour the batter into the two greased pans.

7. Place on a baking sheet for even baking.

8. Place in the oven to bake until cooked through in the middle and slightly brown on the top, about 35 to 40 minutes.

9. Allow to cool before removing from the pan.

10. Mix together the erythritol, lemon juice, heavy cream. Mix well.

11. Pour frosting on top.

12. Serve.

Nutritional Facts Per Serving

- Calories 274
- Fat 23.9g
- Carb 8.1g
- Protein 9g

Donuts

Prep time: 10 minutes | Cook time: 15 minutes | Servings: 12

Ingredients

- Erythritol – ¼ cup
- Flaxseed meal – ¼ cup
- Almond flour – ¾ cup
- Baking powder – 1 tsp.
- Vanilla extract – 1 tsp.
- Eggs – 2
- Coconut oil – 3 tbsp.
- Coconut milk – ¼ cup
- Red food coloring – 20 drops
- Salt – 1 pinch
- Cocoa powder – 1 tbsp.

Method

1. In a bowl, mix erythritol, salt, baking powder, cocoa powder, almond flour, and flaxseed meal. Mix.
2. In another bowl, mix eggs, food coloring, vanilla extract, coconut milk, coconut oil, and mix.

3. Combine 2 mixture well. Pour into a piping bag.
4. Make a hole in the bag and shape 12 doughnuts on a baking sheet.
5. Place in an oven at 350F and bake for 15 minutes.
6. Serve.

Nutritional Facts Per Serving

- Calories: 41
- Protein: 1g
- Carb: 3g
- Fat: 3.7g

Coconut Cake

| Prep time: 20 minutes | Cook time: 50 minutes | Servings: 4 |

Ingredients

- Cream cheese – 4 oz. softened
- Eggs – 3
- Coconut cream – 1 tbsp.
- Sugar-free coconut-flavored syrup – 1 tbsp.
- Coconut flour – 2 tbsp.

For the coconut filling

- Dried unsweetened coconut – 1 cup
- Coconut cream – ½ cup
- Sugar-free coconut-flavored syrup – 3 tbsp.

For the frosting

- Heavy whipping cream – 1 cup
- Sugar-free coconut-flavored syrup – 1 tbsp.
- Stevia powder – 1 tsp.

- Coconut cream – ¼ cup

Method

1. To make the cake: in a blender, combine all of the ingredients and blend until smooth. Let it rest for a few minutes if it is really frothy.

2. Then into a greased 8 x 8 microwave-safe dish, pour ½.

3. Cook in the microwave until firm all the way across, about 3 minutes.

4. Flip out the dish onto a cutting board.

5. Grease again and repeat with the rest of the batter.

6. Cut into squares, so you get 9 squares per pan or 18 squares total.

7. To make the filling: in a bowl, combine all the ingredients and let sit for about ten minutes before using. It will help to absorb all of the liquid.

8. For the frosting: whip the heavy cream before adding the stevia, syrup, and coconut cream. Continue to whip until the cream holds its shape easily.

9. To assemble: on each plate, lay one square of cake and place 1 tbsp. filling in the center of each square.

10. Spread to the edges and then cover with another square of the cake. Repeat until the finish.

11. Use whipped cream to frost the top cake layer and sides.

Nutritional Facts Per Serving

- Calories 543
- Fat 51 g
- Carb 7 g
- Protein 11 g

Cream Cake

Prep time: 45 minutes   Cook time: 45 minutes   Servings: 16

Ingredients

- Butter – ½ cup, softened
- Swerve sweetener – 1 cup
- Eggs – 4, separated
- Heavy cream – ½ cup, room temperature
- Vanilla extract – 1 tsp.
- Almond flour – 1 ½ cups
- Shredded coconut – ½ cup
- Chopped pecans – ½ cup
- Coconut flour – ¼ cup
- Baking powder – 2 tsp.
- Salt – ½ tsp.
- Cream of tartar – ¼ tsp.

Frosting

- Cream cheese – 8 ounces, softened
- Butter – ½ cup, softened

- Powdered Swerve sweetener - 1 cup
- Vanilla extract – 1 tsp.
- Heavy whipping cream – ½ cup

Garnish

- Shredded coconut – 2 tbsp. lightly toasted
- Chopped pecans – 2 tbsp. lightly toasted

Method

1. Grease two round cake pans well and preheat the oven to 325F. Line the pans with parchment paper and then grease the paper.

2. Beat the butter and sweetener in a bowl until combined. One at a time beat in the egg yolks. Now add in the heavy cream and vanilla extract and beat.

3. In another bowl, whisk the salt, almond flour, baking powder, coconut flour, chopped pecans, and shredded coconut. Beat until just combined.

4. Beat the cream of tartar and egg whites in another bowl until stiff peaks form. Then fold into the cake batter.

5. Pour the batter evenly between the pans and spread to the edges.

6. Bake until the cakes are firm to the touch in the middle and golden on the edges, about 35 to 45 minutes.

7. Remove and cool.

8. Frosting: beat butter and cream cheese in a bowl. Beat in the vanilla and sweetener until mixed well.

9. Slowly add the heavy whipping cream.

10. Cover the cake with frosting. Sprinkle the top with pecans and coconut.

11. Cool in the refrigerator for an hour. Slice and serve.

Nutritional Facts Per Serving

- Calories: 335
- Fat: 30.1g
- Carb: 5.7g
- Protein: 5.8g

Conclusion

Thank you again for purchasing this book!

Intermittent fasting is a kind of eating technique that brings about a lot of health benefits to a person's overall health. When done right, it's an incredibly effective therapeutic approach that produces amazing results. If you have been thinking about using fasting to lose weight and get in shape but don't know how then you have come to the right place. This intermittent fasting book is your indispensable guide to simple yet effective weight loss. This guide will change the way you view food, eating time, and weight loss.

I hope this book provided you with a good introduction to the benefits of intermittent fasting. And for those that are more advanced, I hope this provided you with more knowledge and a few new, simple and tasty recipes for you to try.

Please leave a review!

A lot of research and work goes into our books to make the content the best quality for you – our customers. Therefore, we would love it if you left us a review on Amazon! Please go to:

http://www.amazon.com/review/create-review?&asin=B087QR2Z9H

Any comments would be greatly appreciated. We take all comments very seriously and use these comments to update the content and quality of our books for.

Book 2: Keto for Women Over 50

Simple 30 Minute Recipes for Instant Weight Loss and Healthy Living

By Karen Corcoran
2nd Edition

Would you like immediate access to a FREE BOOK? kick start your weight loss journey by transforming your body into a 24/7 fat burning machine!

Ketogenic Diet 101 → Click here to access

Introduction

I want to personally thank you and congratulate you for purchasing this book *"Keto for Women Over 50: Simple 30 minute Keto Recipes for Instant Weight Loss and Healthy Living"*.

Do you ever ask yourself these questions? "Why can't I lose weight like I used to in my twenties?" or "why does healthy food have to taste so boring?" Or, do you ever say this "I don't have time to cook dinner tonight - let's get take out" or "our friends are coming around this weekend and I have no idea what to cook". If so then this book is definitely for you!

The ketogenic diet is a low-carb, high-fat way of eating that has proven to be remarkably effective at transforming people's lives. The ketogenic diet is not just a diet —it is a healthy, weight-reducing way of life. This diet can help you to not only lose weight but control blood pressure, increase mental focus, boost energy, and improve overall health. Keto success is achieved by following low-carb principles. However, finding simple to prep, tasty and easy to cook keto recipes can be difficult. Figuring out what to make on busy days can sometimes seem impossible.

This keto cookbook is specially designed for women over 50 who want to eat up, slim down and reap the health benefits of following a ketogenic lifestyle. All of the following recipes can be cooked in under 30 minutes and are made with good wholesome ingredients. Whether you are new to keto or have experience with keto, these recipes will surprise you. If you want to go keto, but do not know where to start, then this is your go to guide Start to lose weight and gain a healthy lifestyle today!

Thanks again for purchasing this book, I hope you enjoy it!

Chapter One: What is the Ketogenic Diet?

The ketogenic diet has gained popularity during the last few years because it has helped people to lose weight while establishing many health benefits. When you follow a keto diet, it pushes your body into a state known as ketosis. In ketosis, the body creates a different fuel source (ketones) to provide energy for the body. Your body uses glucose as a primary source of energy with a carb-rich diet. With a low-carb diet, your body uses fat as the main source of energy.

Your body does not immediately get into ketosis once you start on the Ketogenic diet. It takes several days to do so. The time depends on the individual. By drastically restricting the carbs, your body burns the fats you consume and fat storage instead of glucose. This happens because your liver converts the fats into fatty acids, and the ketone bodies replace glucose as your energy source. This process is known as ketosis, and it is the goal of the ketogenic diet.

The State of Ketosis

Ketosis is a metabolic process or state where the body uses fats and ketones as its main fuel source instead of glucose. The process of ketosis takes place when fats breakdown into energy in the same way as carbohydrates breakdown to produce glucose to fuel the body.

A ketogenic diet is high in fat, moderate in protein, and low in carbs.

High Fat

The standard keto diet consists of 70 to 75% healthy fats. A high-fat ratio makes keto fun and sustainable for the long term. Once you are fat-adapted, your appetite will reduce naturally because of the high levels of fat you are consuming.

Moderate Protein

A keto diet is made up of about 20 to 25% protein. Eating a moderate amount of protein keeps you full and satisfied. However, you cannot eat too much protein because your body can convert it to glucose.

Low Carb

A Ketogenic diet contains around 5% carb. A standard American diet usually comprises 50 - 60% carbs, so there is a big difference. You need to eat 20 to 50 net carbs a day to stay in ketosis.

Chapter Two: Why Go Keto?

Let's talk about the benefits of going keto.

Helps you prevent and manage diabetes

A carb-rich diet increases your blood sugar levels. An increase in blood sugar level triggers the release of insulin. Gradually, your cells become resistant to insulin, and you develop diabetes. With keto, you drastically limit your carbs and sugars consumption. Both of them trigger a blood sugar spike. With limited blood sugar, your body does not need to release insulin to manage it. Thus, you prevent developing diabetes symptoms. If you already have it, the diet helps you to manage it.

Weight loss

With a ketogenic diet, fat burning is significant because fat-storing hormone insulin production decreases. This makes it easy for the body to access stored body fats and use them as energy.

Appetite control

The Keto diet lowers your appetite. With this diet, your body gets access to months of stored energy, which results in an appetite reduction. Additionally, you consume a high-fat diet with keto. Fats make you feel full quickly and keep you full for a longer period of time.

Lowers your risk of heart disease

The ketogenic diet lowers several risk factors for heart disease, including blood pressure, blood fat percentage, and bad cholesterol. It also increases good cholesterol, improves blood sugar levels and insulin levels. All these jointly lower your risk of heart disease.

More energy and improved mental performance

The keto diet provides your body and brain with a stable fuel source – ketones. The diet prevents sugar swings that are associated with a carb-rich diet. This allows you to avoid brain fog, improves your focus, concentration, and mental clarity.

Boosts brain functions

Your brain health is directly linked with your mental performance and productivity. Research shows that a diet rich in good fats increases brain functions and lowers the risk of mental diseases. The ketogenic diet encourages the consumption of a high amount of omega-3 and omega-6 fatty acids. Both of these are essential for brain health. Natural sources of omega-3 and omega-6 fatty acids include eggs, fish, animal fats, avocados, butter, olive oil, and coconut oil.

Helps to reduce the risk of cancer

Using the keto diet as a cancer treatment and prevention mechanism is gaining popularity. Most of the cancer cells use glucose to survive, and this is why many cancer patients revealed that they felt better once they started a ketogenic diet.

Some health conditions make it difficult for you to follow the diet, including:

People who are naturally very thin

People who are prone to kidney stones

People who have developed a pancreatic problem

People with anorexia

Women who are pregnant or breastfeeding

People with rare metabolic disorders

People with gallbladder disease

Possible Keto side effects and solutions

The diet can cause a few side effects as follows.

Induction Flu: Symptoms include confusion, brain fog, irritability, lethargy, and nausea. These symptoms are common during the first week of the diet.

The cure: consume salt and water. You can cure all these symptoms by getting enough water and salt into your system. Drinking broth daily is a better option.

Leg Cramps: Leg cramps are painful.

The cure: get enough salt and drink plenty of fluids. Taking magnesium supplements is also a good idea. Take three slow release magnesium tablets daily for the first three weeks.

Constipation: Constipation is another side effect of the diet.

The cure: Getting enough salt and water. Also, include more fiber in your diet, such as fruits and vegetables.

Bad Breath: Bad breath is another unpleasant problem that may arise.

The cure:

- Eat more carbohydrates.
- Get enough salt and drink enough fluids
- Maintain good oral hygiene.

Heart palpitations

The cure: getting enough fluid is the easiest solution

Generally, you can eliminate all the Keto side effects by:

- Drinking more water
- Increasing salt intake
- Eating enough fat

Important Disclaimer: the ketogenic lifestyle may not be suitable for all individuals. Please seek professional advice from your doctor or health care professional before adopting this diet or any diet. The author of this book is not a trained medical professional and is not trained to provide medical advice.

Chapter 3 Breakfast Recipes

Sweet Blueberry Pancakes

Prep time: 10 minutes, Cook time: 10 minutes, Servings: 5

Ingredients

- Blueberries – ¼ cup
- Stevia powder – ¼ to ½ tsp.
- Baking powder – 1 tsp.
- Salt – ¼ tsp.
- Golden flaxseed meal – ½ cup
- Almond flour – 1 cup
- Unsweetened almond milk – ¼ cup
- Vanilla extract – ½ tsp.
- Ricotta – ¾ cup
- Eggs – 3

Method

1. Preheat the skillet. In a bowl, blend the vanilla extract, milk, ricotta, and eggs.
2. In another bowl, mix almond flour, golden flaxseed meal, baking powder, stevia, and salt.
3. Blend the dry ingredients into a smooth batter with a hand mixer. Add 2 to 3 blueberries per pancake.

4. Add the butter to the preheated skillet and let the butter melt.

5. Pour the batter into the skillet and flip it when lightly browned on the outside. Cook both sides and repeat with the remaining batter.

6. Serve with additional berries. TIP: mix berries in blender until you have a bright berry sauce.

Nutritional Facts Per Serving *

- Calorie 296.6o Fat 22.6g
- Carb 5.9g
- Protein 13.4g

* PLEASE NOTE: macros and calories for each recipe may vary depending on the brand of the ingredients you use. For more precise macro calculations, use this recipe nutrition calculator found on the My Fitness Pal app and website: https://www.myfitnesspal.com/recipe/calculator.

Also, if you are unsure how many calories you should be eating in a day, please refer to https://www.calculator.net/calorie-calculator.html and enter in your age, height, weight and level of physical activity to understand how many calories you should be eating in one day.

Keto Style Bacon & Eggs

Prep time: 5 minutes, Cook time: 20 minutes, Servings: 2

Ingredients

- Eggs – 3
- Heavy whipping cream – 1/3 cup
- Butter – 1 tbsp.
- Bacon – 4 slices
- Pinch of salt
- Pinch of ground black pepper

Method

1. Preheat the oven to 350F.
2. Place the bacon slices on a cookie sheet.
3. Bake in the oven until crispy, about 10 to 15 minutes.
4. To cook the eggs: in a bowl, whisk the eggs and cream.
5. Heat butter on a pan and add the eggs.
6. Cook the eggs and remove them from the pan.
7. Season with salt and pepper and serve.

Nutritional Facts Per Serving

Calories: 380

- Fat: 34g
- Carb: 1.8g
- Protein: 17g

Keto Porridge

Prep time: 5 minutes, Cook time: 10 minutes, Servings: 1

Ingredients

- Ground cinnamon – 1 tsp.
- Nutmeg – 1 pinch
- Almonds – ½ cup, ground
- Stevia – 1 tsp.
- Coconut cream – ¾ cup
- A pinch of ground cardamom
- A pinch of ground clovesNote: Vegetarian-friendly, keto-friendly.

Method

1. Heat a pan over medium heat. Add coconut cream and heat for a few minutes.
2. Add almonds and stevia. Mix well and cook for 5 minutes.
3. Add cinnamon, nutmeg, cardamom, and cloves. Mix well.
4. Transfer to a bowl and serve.

Nutritional Facts Per Serving

- Calories: 495
- Fat: 66.7g
- Carb: 2.2g

- Protein: 14.3g

Eggs Baked in Avocados

Prep time: 10 minutes, Cook time: 20 minutes, Servings: 4

Ingredients

- Avocados – 2, cut in half and pitted
- Eggs - 4
- Salt and ground black pepper to taste
- Fresh chives – 1 tbsp. chopped

Method

1. Scoop some flesh from the avocado halves and arrange on a baking dish.
2. Crack an egg in each avocado, season with salt, and pepper.
3. Place in the oven at 425F. Bake for 20 minutes.
4. Sprinkle chives and serve. TIP: you may want to also sprinkle on some parmesan cheese if you have this.

Nutritional Facts Per Serving

- Calories: 268
- Fat: 24g
- Carb: 9g
- Protein: 7.5g

Chapter 4 Lunch Recipes

Chicken Sandwich

Prep time: 10 minutes, Cook time: 25 minutes, Servings: 2

Ingredients (bread)

- Eggs – 3
- Cream cheese – 3 oz.
- Cream of tartar – 1/8 tsp.
- Salt and garlic powder

Ingredients (filling)

- Mayonnaise – 1 tbsp.
- Sriracha – 1 tsp.
- Bacon – 2 slices
- Chicken – 3 oz.
- Pepper jack cheese – 2 slices
- Grape tomatoes – 2
- Avocado – ¼

Method

1. Separate the eggs in different bowls. In the egg whites, add cream of tartar, salt, and beat until stiff peaks form.
2. In another bowl, beat the egg yolks with cream cheese.

3. Incorporate the mixture into the egg white mixture and combine carefully.

4. Place the batter on a parchment paper and form little square shapes that look like bread slices.

5. Sprinkle garlic powder on top and bake at 300F for 25 minutes.

6. Meanwhile, cook the chicken and bacon in a pan. Season to taste.

7. When the bread is done, remove from the oven and cool.

8. Make a sandwich with the cooked chicken and bacon, adding the sriracha, mayo, tomatoes, cheese, and mashed avocado to taste.

Nutritional Facts Per Serving

- Calories: 360
- Fat: 28g
- Carb: 3g
- Protein: 22g

Meatballs with Bacon and Cheese

Prep time: 5 minutes, Cook time: 15 minutes, Servings: 5

Ingredients

- Ground beef – 1 ½ lb.
- Pork rinds – ¾ cup, crushed to powder
- Salt – ¾ tsp.
- Pepper – ¾ tsp.
- Cumin – ¾ tsp.
- Garlic powder – ¾ tsp.
- Cheddar cheese – ¾ cup
- Bacon – 4 slices, chopped
- Egg – 1

Method

1. Mix the pork rinds, ground beef, cumin, garlic powder, salt, and pepper. Add the cheese and mix well.
2. Fry the bacon pieces in a hot pan until cooked. Cool.
3. Add the bacon to the meat and combine well. Make meatballs.
4. Cook the meatballs in the pan, browning them on all sides, then cover with a lid for 10 minutes.

5. When finished, let them sit for 5 minutes.
6. Top with the sauce of your choice and serve.

Nutritional Facts Per Serving

- Calories: 450
- Fat: 26g
- Carb: 3g
- Protein: 50g

Steak Salad

Prep time: 10 minutes, Cook time: 20 minutes, Servings: 4

Ingredients

- Steak – 1 ½ pound, sliced thin
- Avocado oil – 3 tbsp.
- Salt and ground black pepper to taste
- Balsamic vinegar – ¼ cup
- Sweet onion – 6 ounces, chopped
- Lettuce head – 1, chopped
- Garlic – 2 cloves, minced
- Mushrooms – 4 ounces, sliced
- Avocado – 1, sliced
- Sundried tomatoes – 3 ounces, cored, and chopped
- Yellow bell pepper – 1, seeded and sliced
- Orange bell pepper – 1, seeded and sliced
- Italian seasoning – 1 tsp.
- Red pepper flakes – 1 tsp.
- Onion powder - 1 tsp.

Method

1. In a bowl, mix steak pieces with vinegar, salt, and pepper. Toss to coat and set aside.
2. Heat a pan with the avocado oil.
3. Add mushrooms, garlic, salt, pepper, onion. Stir-fry for 20 minutes.
4. In a bowl, mix lettuce leaves with bell peppers, avocado, sundried tomatoes, and stir.
5. Season steak pieces with Italian seasoning, pepper flakes, and onion powder.
6. Place steak pieces in a broiling pan, place under a preheated broiler and cook for 5 minutes.
7. Divide the steak pieces on plates; add avocado and lettuce salad on the side.
8. Top everything with onion and mushroom mixture.
9. Serve.

Nutritional Facts Per Serving

- Calories: 516
- Fat: 50.1g
- Carb: 5.3g
- Protein: 23.1g

Almond Pizza

Prep time: 5 minutes, Cook time: 12 minutes, Servings: 4

Ingredients

- Almond meal – ¾ cup
- Baking powder – 1 ½ tsp.
- Granulated sweetener – 1 ½ tsp.
- Oregano – ½ tsp.
- Thyme – ¼ tsp.
- Garlic powder – ½ tsp.
- Eggs – 2
- Butter – 5 tbsp.
- Alfredo sauce – ½ cup
- Cheddar cheese – 4 oz.

Method

1. Mix the dry ingredients in a bowl.
2. Add the eggs to the dry mixture.
3. Melt the butter and incorporate it.
4. On a greased pizza pan, spread the crust and pre-cook at 350F for 7 minutes.
5. Remove from the oven and spread the Alfredo sauce and

cheddar cheese on top.

6. Cook 5 minutes more and serve.

Nutritional Facts Per Serving

- Calories: 460
- Fat: 45g
- Carb: 5g
- Protein: 15g

Chapter 5 Dinner Recipes

Shrimp & Bacon Chowder

Prep time: 5 minutes, Cook time: 25 minutes, Servings: 6

Ingredients

- Bacon – 6 slices, chopped
- Medium turnip – 1, cut into ½ cubes
- Chopped onion – ½ cup
- Garlic – 2 cloves, minced
- Chicken broth – 2 cups
- Heavy whipping cream – 1 cup
- Shrimp – 1 pound, peeled and deveined
- Cajun seasoning – ½ tsp.
- Salt and pepper
- Chopped parsley for garnish

Method

1. Cook bacon in a Dutch oven until crisp. Remove and drain on paper towels. Reserve the bacon fat in the pan.
2. Add the onion and turnip and sauté for 5 minutes, or until onion is tender. Add garlic and cook until fragrant.
3. Pour in chicken broth and simmer for 10 minutes.
4. Add shrimp and cream and simmer for another 3 minutes, or until shrimp is cooked through.

5. Add Cajun seasoning and season with salt and pepper.
6. Garnish with chopped parsley and bacon and serve.

Nutritional Facts Per Serving

- Calories: 391
- Fat: 31.1g
- Carb: 5.6g
- Protein: 16.5g

Creamy Salmon

Prep time: 10 minutes, Cook time: 20 minutes, Servings: 6

Ingredients

- Olive oil – 2 Tbsp.
- Salmon fillets – 3 (6-ounce)
- Garlic – 2 cloves, minced
- Heavy whipping cream – 1 cup
- Cream cheese – 1 ounce
- Capers – 2 Tbsp.
- Lemon juice – 1 Tbsp.
- Fresh dill – 2 tsp.
- Grated Parmesan cheese – 2 Tbsp.

Method

1. Heat oil in a skillet. Add the salmon and search each side for 5 minutes.
2. Once cooked, remove and set aside.
3. Add the minced garlic to the pan and sauté until fragrant.
4. Add the capers, lemon juice, cream cheese, and heavy cream to the pan.
5. Bring to a light simmer. Stir frequently.

6. Once the sauce starts to thicken, add the salmon back in the pan. Coat the salmon with the sauce and just reheat the fish.

7. Garnish with Parmesan cheese and fresh dill and serve.

Nutritional Facts Per Serving

- Calories: 494
- Fat: 30.67g
- Carb: 2.15g
- Protein: 53.56g

Orange Chicken

Prep time: 10 minutes, Cook time: 15 minutes, Servings: 4

Ingredients (chicken)

- Chicken thighs – 2 pounds, skinless, boneless, and cut into pieces
- Salt and ground black pepper to taste
- Coconut oil – 3 Tbsp.
- Coconut flour – ¼ cup

Ingredients (sauce)

- Fish sauce – 2 Tbsp.
- Lemon zest – 1 ½ tsp.
- Fresh ginger - 1 Tbsp. grated
- Orange juice – ¼ cup, no sugar added
- Stevia – 2 tsp.
- Sesame seeds – ¼ tsp.
- Scallions – 2 Tbsp. chopped
- Coriander – ½ tsp.
- Water – 1 cup

- Red pepper flakes – ¼ tsp.
- Liquid aminos – 2 Tbsp.

Method

1. In a bowl, mix coconut flour, salt, pepper, and stir.
2. Add chicken pieces and toss to coat well.
3. Heat a pan with oil. Add chicken, and cook until golden brown on both sides. Transfer to a bowl.
4. In a blender, mix orange juice with ginger, fish sauce, liquid aminos, stevia, lemon zest, water, coriander, and blend well.
5. Pour into a pan and heat over medium heat.
6. Add chicken, stir, and cook for 2 minutes.
7. Add sesame seeds, scallions, and pepper flakes. Stir-fry for 2 minutes. Remove from heat.
8. Serve.

Nutritional Facts Per Serving

- Calories: 542
- Fat: 27.4g
- Carb: 4.3g
- Protein: 65g

Duck with Sauce

Prep time: 5 minutes, Cook time: 25 minutes, Servings: 2

Ingredients (duck)

- Duck breasts – 2
- Salt – 1 tsp.
- Pepper – ½ tsp.
- Chinese 5 spice – 1.5 tsp.

Ingredients (sauce)

- Chicken stock – 1 cup
- Xylitol – 2 Tbsp.
- Tamari – 4 Tbsp.
- Chinese 5 spice – ½ tsp.
- Cinnamon – ½ tsp.
- Apple cider vinegar – 2 tsp.
- Peel of one orange

Method

1. Preheat the oven to 400F.
2. Combine all the sauce ingredients in a small saucepan.
3. Simmer the sauce for 20 to 25 minutes on low heat while you prepare the duck. Whisk occasionally.
4. To prepare the duck, combine salt, pepper, and 5 spice.

5. Score the duck skin (similar to crisscross pattern).
6. Rub the duck breast well with the spice mixture.
7. Heat a pan and place the duck breasts, skin side down.
8. Cook for 5 minutes, then turn and cook for 2 minutes more. Drain off the fat.
9. Cook the duck in the oven for 8 to 10 minutes.
10. Remove from the oven. Cover with a foil and rest. Discard the orange peel.
11. Serve with a salad.

Nutritional Facts Per Serving

- Calories: 358
- Fat: 11g
- Carb: 9g
- Protein: 52g

Pan-Seared Steak

Prep time: 5 minutes, Cook time: 10 minutes, Servings: 1

Ingredients

- Steak (filet, sirloin strip, ribeye) – 6 oz. (about 1 inch thick)
- Salted butter – 2 Tbsp.
- Sliced shiitake mushrooms – ½ cup
- Kosher salt and pepper to taste

Method

1. Heat a cast-iron pan on medium heat for 1 minute.
2. Season the steak with salt and pepper and add to the hot pan.
3. Cook 3 to 4 minutes for medium-rare.
4. Remove the steak to a plate.
5. Add butter and mushrooms to the pan.
6. Cook until the mushrooms are golden brown, about 3 to 4 minutes. Remove from the heat.
7. Season the mushroom with salt and pepper if needed.
8. Add the steak back to the pan and baste in the butter.
9. Allow to rest in the warm butter for a couple of minutes.
10. Slice and serve.

Nutritional Facts Per Serving

- Calories 370
- Fat 29g
- Carb 3g
- Protein 35g

Chapter 6 Vegetarian Recipes

Spinach Soup

Prep time: 10 minutes, Cook time: 15 minutes, Servings: 8

Ingredients

- Butter – 2 tbsp.
- Spinach – 20 ounces, chopped
- Garlic – 1 tsp. minced
- Salt and ground black pepper to taste
- Chicken stock – 45 ounces
- Ground nutmeg – ½ tsp.
- Heavy cream – 2 cups
- Onion – 1, chopped

Method

1. Heat a saucepan and melt the butter.
2. Add onion, and stir-fry for 4 minutes.
3. Add garlic, and stir-fry for 1 minute.
4. Add spinach and stock, and stir-fry for 5 minutes. Remove from heat.
5. Blend soup with a hand mixer and heat the soup again.

6. Add salt, pepper, nutmeg, cream, stir, and cook for 5 minutes.

7. Serve.

Nutritional Facts Per Serving

- Calories: 158
- Fat: 14.7g
- Carb: 5.4g
- Protein: 3.3g

Asparagus Frittata

Prep time: 10 minutes, Cook time: 15 minutes, Servings: 4

Ingredients

- Onion – ¼ cup, chopped
- A drizzle of olive oil
- Asparagus spears – 1-pound, cut into 1-inch pieces
- Salt and ground black pepper to taste
- Eggs – 4, whisked
- Cheddar cheese – 1 cup, grated

Method

1. Heat a pan with oil over medium heat.
2. Add onions, and stir-fry for 3 minutes.
3. Add asparagus and stir-fry for 6 minutes.
4. Add eggs and stir-fry for 3 minutes.
5. Add salt, pepper, and sprinkle with cheese.
6. Place in the oven and broil for 3 minutes.
7. Divide frittata on plates and serve.

Nutritional Facts Per Serving

- Calories: 202
- Fat: 13.3g

- Carb: 5.8g
- Protein: 15.1g

Bell Peppers Soup

Prep time: 10 minutes, Cook time: 15 minutes, Servings: 6

Ingredients

- Roasted bell peppers – 12, seeded and chopped
- Olive oil – 2 tbsp.
- Garlic – 2 cloves, minced
- Vegetable stock – 30 ounces
- Salt and black pepper to taste
- Water - 6 ounces
- Heavy cream – 2/3 cup
- Onion – 1, chopped
- Parmesan cheese – ¼ cup, grated
- Celery stalks – 2, chopped

Method

1. Heat a saucepan with oil over medium heat.
2. Add onion, garlic, celery, salt, and pepper. Stir-fry for 8 minutes.
3. Add water, bell peppers, stock, stir, and bring to a boil. Cover, lower heat, and simmer for 5 minutes.
4. Remove from heat and blend with a hand mixer.

5. Then adjust seasoning, and add cream. Stir and bring to a boil.

6. Remove from the heat and serve on bowls.

7. Sprinkle with Parmesan and serve.

Nutritional Facts Per Serving

- Calories: 155
- Fat: 12g
- Carb: 8.6g
- Protein: 4.7g

Radish Hash Browns

Prep time: 10 minutes, Cook time: 10 minutes, Servings: 4

Ingredients

- Onion powder – ½ tsp.
- Radishes – 1 pound, shredded
- Garlic powder – ½ tsp.
- Salt and ground black pepper to taste
- Eggs – 4
- Parmesan cheese – 1/3 cup, grated

Method

1. In a bowl, mix radishes, with salt, pepper, onion, garlic powder, eggs, Parmesan cheese, and mix well.
2. Spread on a lined baking sheet.
3. Place in an oven at 375F and bake for 10 minutes.
4. Serve.

Nutritional Facts Per Serving

- Calories: 104
- Fat: 6g
- Carb: 4.5g
- Protein: 8.6g

Chapter 7 Vegan Recipes

Celery Soup

Prep time: 10 minutes, Cook time: 30 minutes, Servings: 6

Ingredients

- Celery – 1 bunch, chopped
- Onion – 1, chopped
- Green onion – 1 bunch, chopped
- Garlic cloves – 4, minced
- Salt and ground black pepper to taste
- Parsley – 1 fresh bunch, chopped
- Fresh mint bunches – 2, chopped
- Persian lemons – 3 dried, pricked with a fork
- Water – 2 cups
- Olive oil – 4 Tbsp.

Method

1. Heat a saucepan with oil over medium heat.
2. Add onion, garlic, and green onions. Stir and cook for 6 minutes.
3. Add Persian lemons, celery, salt, pepper, water, stir, cover

pan, and simmer on medium heat for 20 minutes.
4. Add parsley and mint, stir, and cook for 10 minutes.
5. Blend with a hand mixer and serve.

Nutritional Facts Per Serving

- Calories: 100
- Fat: 9.5g
- Carb: 4.4g
- Protein: 1g

Spring Greens Soup

Prep time: 10 minutes Cook time: 30 minutes Servings: 4

Ingredients

- Mustard greens – 2 cups, chopped
- Collard greens – 2 cups, chopped
- Vegetable stock – 4 cups
- Onion – 1, chopped
- Salt and ground black pepper to taste
- Coconut amions – 2 Tbsp.
- Fresh ginger – 2 tsp. grated

Method

6. Put the stock into a saucepan and bring to a simmer over medium heat.
7. Add ginger, coconut aminos, salt, pepper, onion, mustard, and collard greens. Stir, cover, and cook for 30 minutes. Remove from the heat.
8. Blend the soup with a hand mixer.
9. Serve.

Nutritional Facts Per Serving

- Calories: 35
- Fat: 1g
- Carb: 7g
- Protein: 2g

Alfalfa Sprouts Salad

Prep time: 10 minutes, Cook time: 10 minutes, Servings: 4

Ingredients

- Dark sesame oil – 1 ½ tsp.
- Alfalfa sprouts – 4 cups
- Salt and ground black pepper to taste
- Grapeseed oil – 1 ½ tsp.
- Coconut yogurt – ¼ cup

Method

1. In a bowl, mix sprouts with yogurt, grape seed oil, sesame oil, salt, and pepper. Toss to coat and serve.

Nutritional Facts Per Serving

- Calories: 83
- Fat: 7.6g
- Carb: 3.4g
- Protein: 1.6g

Eggplant Stew

Prep time: 10 minutes Cook time: 30 minutes Servings: 4

Ingredients

- Onion – 1, chopped
- Garlic – 2 cloves, chopped
- Fresh parsley – 1 bunch, chopped
- Salt and black pepper to taste
- Dried oregano – 1 tsp.
- Eggplants – 2, cut into chunks
- Olive oil – 2 Tbsp.
- Capers – 2 Tbsp. chopped
- Green olives – 12, pitted and sliced
- Tomatoes – 5, chopped
- Herb vinegar – 3 Tbsp.

Method

1. In a saucepan, heat oil over medium heat.
2. Add oregano, eggplant, salt, pepper, and stir-fry for 5 minutes.
3. Add parsley, onion, garlic, and stir-fry for 4 minutes.
4. Add tomatoes, vinegar, olives, capers, and stir-fry for 15

minutes.
5. Adjust seasoning and stir.
6. Serve.

Nutritional Facts Per Serving
- Calories: 280
- Fat: 17.9g
- Carb: 8.4g
- Protein: 5.4g

Chapter 8 Desserts (NEW Bonus Chapter!)

Almond Cookies

Prep time: 10 minutes   Cook time: 20 minutes   Servings: 18

Ingredients

- Almond butter – 2 tbsp.
- Coconut oil – 1 tbsp.
- Coconut milk – ¼ cup
- Sugar-free coconut syrup – 2 tbsp.
- Eggs – 2 large
- Baking powder – ½ tsp.
- Salt – ½ tsp.
- Granulated sugar substitute – 2 tbsp.
- Sugar-free dried coconut – 1 ½ cup
- Flax meal – ½ cup
- 90% dark chocolate – 2 squares
- Almonds – 18

Method

1. In a bowl, combine the coconut oil and almond butter and mix well.

2. Add the eggs, syrup, and coconut milk and mix until smooth.

3. Stir in the flax meal, dried coconut, sweetener, salt, and baking powder.

4. Roll the dough into 18 (1-inch) balls and place on a parchment covered cookie sheet.

5. Press lightly to make a dent on each ball.

6. Top with chopped chocolate (each cookie) and top with an almond.

7. Bake in a preheated 375F/190C oven until browned and slightly puffed, about 20 minutes.

8. Serve.

Nutritional Facts Per Serving

- Calories 114
- Fat 11g
- Carb 4g
- Protein 3g

Pumpkin Pie Cupcakes

Prep time: 15 minutes, Cook time: 30 minutes, Servings: 6

Ingredients

- Coconut flour – 3 Tbsp.
- Pumpkin pie spice – 1 tsp.
- Baking powder – ¼ tsp.
- Baking soda – ¼ tsp.
- Pinch salt
- Pumpkin puree – ¾ cup
- Swerve brown – 1/3 cup
- Heavy whipping cream – ¼ cup
- Egg – 1
- Vanilla – ½ tsp.

Method

1. Line 6 muffin cups with parchment paper and preheat the oven to 350F.
2. In a bowl, whisk together the salt, baking soda, baking powder, pumpkin pie spice, and coconut flour.
3. In another bowl, whisk egg, vanilla, cream, sweetener, and pumpkin puree until mixed. Whisk in dry ingredients.
4. Pour into the muffin cups and bake until just puffed and almost set, about 25 to 30 minutes.

5. Remove and cool.
6. Refrigerate for about 1 hour.
7. Top with whipped cream and serve.

Nutritional Facts Per Serving

- Calories: 70
- Fat: 4.1g
- Carb: 5.1g
- Protein: 1.7g

Brownies

Prep time: 15 minutes, cook time: 20 minutes, Servings: 16

Ingredients

- Butter – ½ cup, melted
- Swerve sweetener – 2/3 cup
- Eggs – 3
- Vanilla extract – ½ tsp.
- Almond flour – ½ cup
- Cocoa powder – 1/3 cup
- Gelatin – 1 Tbsp.
- Baking powder – ½ tsp.
- Salt – ¼ tsp.
- Water – ¼ cup
- Sugar-free chocolate chips – 1/3 cup

Method

1. Grease a (8 x 8-inch) baking pan and preheat the oven to 350F.
2. In a bowl, whisk together eggs, vanilla extract, sweetener, and butter.
3. Add the salt, baking powder, gelatin, cocoa powder, and flour and whisk until combined. Stir in the chocolate chips.
4. Fill the prepared baking pan with the batter.

5. Bake until center still a bit wet, but the edges are set, about 15 to 20 minutes.

6. Remove, cool, slice, and serve.

Nutritional Facts Per Serving

- Calories: 110
- Fat: 9.5g
- Carb: 3.6g
- Protein: 3.1g

Ice Cream

Prep time: 15 minutes Cook time: 30 minutes Servings: 8

Ingredients

- Heavy whipping cream – 2 ½ cups, divided
- Swerve brown – ¼ cup
- Sugar substitute – ¼ cup
- Butter – 2 Tbsp.
- Maple extract – 1 ½ tsp.
- Xanthan gum – ¼ tsp.
- Chopped walnuts – 1/3 cup

Method

1. In a saucepan, bring two sweeteners, and 1 ¼ cups of the whipping cream to a simmer. Lower heat and gently simmer for 30 minutes.
2. Remove from the heat and whisk in maple extract, and butter. Add the xanthan gum and whisk to mix well. Cool, then place in the refrigerator for about 2 hours.
3. Beat the remaining whipping cream in a bowl until stiff peaks. Foil in chilled cream/maple until well combined. Stir in chopped walnuts.
4. Freeze until firm.
5. Serve.

Nutritional Facts Per Serving

- Calories: 318
- Fat: 31.7g
- Carb: 2.9g
- Protein: 2.8g

Chapter 9 Snack Recipes (NEW Bonus Chapter!)

Parmesan Crackers

Prep time: 10 minutes, Cook time: 5 minutes, Servings: 8

Ingredients

- Butter – 1 tsp.
- Full-fat parmesan – 8 ounces, shredded

Method

1. Preheat the oven to 400F.
2. Line a baking sheet with parchment paper and lightly grease the paper with the butter.
3. Spoon the parmesan cheese onto the baking sheet in mounds, spread evenly apart.
4. Spread out the mounds with the back of a spoon until they are flat.
5. Bake about 5 minutes, or until the center are still pale, and edges are browned.
6. Remove, cool, and serve.

Nutritional Facts Per Serving

- Calories: 133
- Fat: 11g
- Carb: 1g

- Protein: 11g

Deviled Eggs

Prep time: 15 minutes Cook time: 10 minutes Servings: 12

Ingredients

- Large eggs – 6, hardboiled, peeled, and halved lengthwise
- Creamy mayonnaise – ¼ cup
- Avocado – ¼, chopped
- Swiss cheese – ¼ cup, shredded
- Dijon mustard – ½ tsp.
- Ground black pepper
- Bacon slices – 6, cooked and chopped

Method

1. Remove the yolks and place them in a bowl. Place the whites on a plate, hollow-side up.
2. Mash the yolks with a fork and add Dijon mustard, cheese, avocado, and mayonnaise. Mix well and season yolk mixture with the black pepper.
3. Spoon the yolk mixture back into the egg white hollows and top each egg half with the chopped bacon.
4. Serve.

Nutritional Facts Per Serving

- Calories: 85
- Fat: 7g

- Carb: 2g
- Protein: 6g

Almond Garlic Crackers

Prep time: 10 minutes, Cook time: 15 minutes, Servings: 4

Ingredients

- Almond flour – ½ cup
- Ground flaxseed – ½ cup
- Shredded Parmesan cheese – 1/3 cup
- Garlic powder – 1 tsp.
- Salt – ½ tsp.
- Water as needed

Method

1. Line a baking sheet with parchment paper and preheat the oven to 400F.
2. In a bowl, mix salt, Parmesan cheese, garlic powder, water, ground flaxseed, and almond meal. Set aside for 3 to 5 minutes.
3. Put dough on the baking sheet and cover with plastic wrap. Flatten the dough with a rolling pin.
4. Remove the plastic wrap and score the dough with a knife to make dents.
5. Bake in the oven for 15 minutes.
6. Remove, cool, and break into individual crackers.

<u>Nutritional Facts Per Serving</u>

- Calories: 96
- Fat: 14g
- Carb: 4g
- Protein: 4g

Fat Bombs

Prep time: 10 minutes, Cook time: 15 minutes, Servings: 6

Ingredients

- Avocado – ½, peeled, and halved
- Butter – ¼ cup
- Garlic – 2 cloves, crushed
- Chili pepper – 1, chopped
- Cilantro – 2 Tbsp. chopped
- Lime juice – 1 Tbsp.
- Onion – ½, diced
- Bacon – 4 slices
- Salt and pepper to taste

Method

1. Preheat the oven to 375F.
2. Cook the bacon strips on a baking tray for 15 minutes. Reserve the grease.
3. Combine the first six ingredients. Season with salt, and pepper, and mix.
4. Add the onion and the bacon grease and mix. Refrigerate for 20 to 30 minutes.
5. Crumble the bacon. Create 6 balls from the mixture.
6. Roll each ball in the bacon crumbles.
7. Serve.

Nutritional Facts Per Serving

- Calories: 156
- Fat: 15.2g
- Carb: 1.4g
- Protein: 3.4g

Chapter 10 - 21 Day Meal Plan (NEW Bonus Chapter!)

Here is a meal plan that you may wish to follow to get yourself started. These recipes have been organized to allow for an easy weekly visit to the grocery store. You can cook some of these meal in batches (e.g. meatballs with bacon and cheese) to save time. Meal prepping takes practice however you will get quicker at this overtime.

You will see here that each week has a select number of recipes with new recipes being introduced in the weeks thereafter. I recommend that you try all recipes in this book to ensure this lifestyle change is as exciting for you as possible.

This meal plan does not include snacks. You will need to eat snacks to keep yourself energized throughout the day and to increase your calorie intake. Some plans below are under 1,200 per day. <u>It is not recommended that you eat below 1,200 calories per day!</u> If you don't have the time to prepare any of the snack recipes, I recommend snacking on roasted almonds (28 almonds = 200 calories) or celery and carrot sticks (tastes great with a spoonful of almond butter).

		Breakfast	Lunch	Dinner	Total Calories
Week 1	Day 1	Keto Style Bacon & Eggs	Almond Pizza	Creamy Salmon	1,334
	DAY 2	Asparagus Frittata	Meatballs with Bacon and Cheese	Orange Chicken	1,194
	DAY 3	Eggs Baked in Avocados	Spinach Soup	Creamy Salmon	920
	DAY 4	Asparagus Frittata	Almond Pizza	Orange Chicken	1,382
	DAY 5	Eggs Baked in Avocados	Meatballs with Bacon and Cheese	Bell Peppers soup	873
	DAY 6	Asparagus Frittata	Spinach Soup	Creamy Salmon	854
	DAY 7	Keto Style Bacon & Eggs	Meatballs with Bacon and Cheese	Bell Peppers soup	985

		Breakfast	**Lunch**	**Dinner**	**Total Calories**
Week 2	DAY 8	Radish Hash Browns	Chicken Sandwich	Shrimp & Bacon Chowder	855
	DAY 9	Sweet Blueberry Pancakes	Steak Salad	Celery Soup	912.5
	DAY 10	Keto Porridge	Eggplant Stew	Pan-Seared Steak	1,145
	DAY 11	Radish Hash Browns	Chicken Sandwich	Shrimp & Bacon Chowder	855
	DAY 12	Sweet Blueberry Pancakes	Steak Salad	Celery Soup	912.5
	DAY 13	Radish Hash Browns	Chicken Sandwich	Shrimp & Bacon Chowder	855
	DAY 14	Keto Porridge	Eggplant Stew	Pan-Seared Steak	1,145

		Breakfast	Lunch	Dinner	Total Calories
Week 3	DAY 15	Keto Style Bacon & Eggs	Bell Peppers Soup	Duck with Sauce	893
	DAY 16	Eggs Baked in Avocados	Almond Pizza	Creamy Salmon	1,222
	DAY 17	Asparagus Frittata	Meatballs with Bacon and Cheese	Steak Salad	1,168
	DAY 18	Keto Style Bacon & Eggs	Bell Peppers Soup	Duck with Sauce	893
	DAY 19	Eggs Baked in Avocados	Almond Pizza	Creamy Salmon	1,222
	DAY 20	Keto Style Bacon & Eggs	Bell Peppers Soup	Duck with Sauce	893
	DAY 21	Asparagus Frittata	Meatballs with Bacon and Cheese	Steak Salad	1,168

Conclusion

Thank you again for purchasing this book!

I hope this book provided you with a good introduction to the benefits of the ketogenic diet. And for those that are more advanced, I hope this provided you with a few new, simple and tasty recipes for you to try and add into your ketogenic lifestyle.

If you're after more keto lifestyle tips and tricks, or if you would like free delicious recipes, please like our **Facebook page - 30 Minute Keto Recipes for Instant Weight Loss and Healthy Living.**

Please leave a review!

A lot of research and work goes into our books to make the content the best quality for you – our customers. Therefore, we would love it if you left us a review on Amazon! Please go to:

http://www.amazon.com/review/create-review?&asin=B087QR2Z9H

Any comments would be greatly appreciated. We take all comments very seriously and use these comments to update the content and quality of our books for.

Book 3: An Instant Pot Will Save Your Life...!

Simple 4-Ingredient Recipes for Busy People

By Karen Corcoran
2nd Edition

Would you like immediate access to a **FREE EBOOK?**

[Click here](#) to access **101 expert cooking tips** for:

- Meal planning
- Useful kitchen gadgets
- Freezing tips

...AND MUCH MORE!

Introduction

I want to personally thank you and congratulate you for purchasing this book "An Instant Pot Will Save Your Life: Simple 4 Ingredient Recipes for Busy People".

Do you ever ask yourself these questions?

"I don't know what to cook"

"I don't know how to cook"

"That recipe will take too long"

Life is busy and chances are you have uttered one or all of these phrases to yourself at some point. After spending the majority of your day at the office, going to class or looking after the kids, cooking a meal that is healthy, tastes good and is budget-friendly might seem impossible and is probably the last thing you want to be doing.

For a lot of us, settling for fast food or dining out at an expensive restaurant almost always seems like the easiest way to go. Despite the fact that doing this chews up our funds and expands our waistlines, this habit can be a difficult one for us to break.

There are a number of disadvantages that accrue to the adoption of this lifestyle, the most prevalent of which is the development of lifestyle diseases such as obesity. This is why having access to healthy, cheap and fast cooking meals is so important for busy professionals, students and families.

Overweight and obese persons generally have very low energy which stops them from living a fulfilling life. Even worse, such persons are more predisposed to mental health disorders such as anxiety, depression, and other cognitive disorders. And with these disorders comes a myriad of problems, ranging from poor self-image to suicidal ideations.

Luckily, a proper diet is only an instant pot away, literally! Instant pots are multi-cookers that serve as steamers, rice cookers, slow cookers, pressure cookers, sauté pans, and warming pots all in one. An instant pot is the best investment that a busy person can make as it saves them from investing in multiple kitchen appliances.

You can buy an instant pot for as little as $70 USD on Amazon. You should shop around on amazon and other online stores to ensure you're getting the best deal. Please note that there are different instant pots however, their functioning is more or less the same so you can use any instant pot to make delicious recipes. Read through the manual to better understand your instant pot model.

When it comes to ingredients, what if I told you that you can make a full healthy and affordable meal with only four ingredients? This cookbook will provide you with breakfast, lunch, dinner, and dessert recipes that only require four ingredients. The major focus of this cookbook is:

- **Nutrition.** The recipes included in this book are nutritious, and we have included a breakdown of the nutritional value for every meal.

- **Cost efficiency**. All ingredients used are affordable and easily available.

- **Time efficiency.** We know how busy you are..! Therefore, we are only including recipes that take between 15-60 minutes. For most of these recipes, you can cook in large batches to save yourself cooking everyday throughout the week.

Cooking does not have to be so hard. Let's begin the journey together! Thanks again for purchasing this book, I hope you enjoy it!

Please leave a review!

A lot of research and work goes into our books to make the content the best quality for you – our customers. Therefore, we would love it if you left us a review on Amazon! Please go to:

http://www.amazon.com/review/create-review?&asin=B087QR2Z9H

Any comments would be greatly appreciated. We take all comments very seriously and use these comments to update the content and quality of our books for.

Chapter One: Breakfast Recipes

Spanish Eggs

Note: Vegetarian-friendly, keto-friendly.

Serving size: 2

Estimated time: 10 -15 minutes

Ingredients

- 2 eggs
- 1 cup baby kale
- 1 tablespoon olive oil
- ½ diced onion

Spices (optional)

- ¼ teaspoon cumin powder
- ¼ teaspoon black pepper powder
- ¼ teaspoon Spanish paprika
- ½ cup marinara sauce
- Salt and pepper to taste

Instructions

1. Turn on the instant pot and select the sauté function.
2. Heat olive oil and fry the onions until golden brown.

3. Add your selected spices, and stir gently for approximately 2 minutes.
4. Add kale and cook until soft. This should take between 1-2 minutes.
5. Add in marinara sauce and season with salt and pepper. Stir to ensure that the three are well mixed together.
6. Turn off the pot and allow it to cool for at least 3 minutes.
7. Open the pot and crack eggs carefully, ensuring that they are evenly spaced. Do not stir the eggs, just crack them on top of the cooked kale mixture.
8. Close the lid and select low-pressure cooking for a duration of 1 minute.
9. Once it beeps, open slowly and be careful not to get burnt by the steam.

Nutritional value per serving

(excludes optionals and toppings)

- Calories: 280
- Total fat: 8.2g
- Saturated fat: 2.0 g
- Carbohydrates: 6.7g
- Protein: 6.8g
- Dietary Fiber: 6.8g
- Sugars: 2g

Coconut Porridge

Note: vegan-friendly, gluten-free, grain-free, dairy-free, nut-free

Serving size: 2

Estimated time: 20 minutes

Ingredients

- 2 tablespoon of shredded coconut
- 3 tablespoons of sunflower seeds (lightly toasted). Can substitute with 2 tablespoons of coconut butter or coconut flakes
- 1 cup of squash (butternut)
- Pure maple syrup/raw honey
- ½ cup water/coconut milk

Spices

- ½ tablespoon cinnamon
- I pinch salt

Toppings (optional)

- Tart cherries
- Blueberries
- Sesame seeds
- Coconut cream

Instructions

1. Chop the squash into large pieces and place into the instant pot. Add 1 tablespoon of coconut oil and a pinch of your preferred spices.
2. Sauté for 5 minutes, turning the squash every minute. The top part should be well coated with the oil.
3. Add 1/3 cup of water into the pressure cooker and lock the lid. Close the pressure valve and cook for 5 minutes.
4. Allow a 10-minute natural pressure release. You can also use the quick release option, particularly when you are pressed with time.
5. Remove the squash and puree with a hand blender.
6. Mix all the other dry ingredients (seeds, shredded coconut, and your preferred spices) in a small bowl. Add milk and stir together.
7. Mix the dry ingredients with the pureed squash, and pour the mixture back into the pot.
8. Heat for 2 minutes, and serve. If you want to keep it warm, place the lid back on and turn the warm mode on until you are ready to serve.

Nutritional value per serving

(excludes optionals and toppings)

- Calories: 331
- Total fat: 17.7g
- Saturated fat: 6.1g
- Carbohydrates: 43.1g
- Sugars: 16g
- Dietary fiber: 8.7g
- Protein: 7g

Choc-Banana Bread

Serving size: 8

Estimated time: 60 min

Ingredients

- 3 small bananas
- 2 eggs
- 1 cup self-raising flour
- ½ cup mini chocolate chips (use cooking chocolate or chocolate that is low in sugar)
- 2 tablespoon canola/vegetable oil

Instructions

1. In a small bowl, mash the small bananas until smooth.
2. Add oil and eggs, stir until fully combined.
3. Add flour and continue stirring. Ensure that there are no white streaks that remain. Add in the chocolate chips and mix thoroughly.
4. Spray a bread pan using a non-stick cooking spray. Pour in the batter and ensure that you smooth it at the top. Since the cake will expand when it begins cooking, ensure the pan is tall enough so there is some space. Then, cover

loosely using a foil to prevent water steam from dripping on top of the cake.
5. Pour 2 cups of water into the instant pot. Place the bread pan on top of the sling and lower it into the instant pot.
6. Cover the pot and make sure that the lid is secure. Ensure that the valve setting is set to sealing, to ensure that the pot is fully covered.
7. Set the timer to 60 minutes and on very high pressure. When it beeps, allow it to release naturally.
8. Remove the lid, lift out the cake pan and let the bread sit for at least 10 minutes to cool. You can run a knife around the edges to loosen it.
9. Invert the pan on a plate. Cut it up as you desire and enjoy.
10. To ensure that any leftovers stay fresh for a long time, store in an airtight container. This bread also freezes very well.

Nutritional value per serving

(excludes optionals and toppings)

- Calories: 313
- Carbohydrates: 39.6g
- Total fat: 16.6g
- Saturated fat: 4.2g
- Sugars: 24.5g
- Protein: 4g
- Dietary fiber: 2g

Banana Nut Oatmeal

Serving size: 3

Estimated time: 30 minutes

Ingredients

- 1 cup of oats
- 2 sliced bananas
- ½ cup sliced almonds
- Maple syrup (optional)
- 3 cups of water
- 1 tablespoon of cinnamon

Instructions

1. Pour water, oats, one chopped banana and cinnamon in the instant pot and give a small stir.
2. Close the lid and seal the vent. Press the manual button and set the timer to 30 minutes.
3. The pressure will come in at about 15 minutes. The countdown will begin and the timer will go off once it is done.
4. Allow the pressure to release naturally. This will take about 10 minutes. If you are in a hurry, you can always allow fast release.

5. Open the lid carefully to prevent steam burns. Scoop the oatmeal and put it into a bowl.
6. Add banana slices, almond, and maple syrup into your bowl.
7. You can add any toppings of your choice.

Nutritional value per serving

(excludes optionals and toppings)

- Calories: 278
- Total Fat: 6g
- Dietary Fiber: 5g
- Protein: 10g
- Carbohydrates: 45g
- Sugar: 15g

Tasty Morning Pancakes

Note: This recipe works best with the Instant Pot 7-in-1 Multi-Functional Pressure Cooker (6-quart version). Other versions tend to cook faster, and it is recommended that you change from manual mode to rice mode.

Serving size: 1

Estimated time: 40 minutes

Ingredients

- 2 cups of all-purpose flour (you can substitute with gluten-free almond flour)
- 2 teaspoons of baking powder
- 2 tablespoons white sugar (or you may want to use stevia as healthier alternative)
- 2 eggs
- 1 ½ cups of milk (can substitute with almond milk)

Instructions

1. In a medium bowl, whisk the eggs and milk together until they are completely mixed. Add in flour, baking powder, and sugar. Whisk until the lumps disappear.

2. Grease the interior of your instant pot thoroughly with cooking spray. Ensure that the bottom has a few extra layers of the coating, to ensure that the pancake does not get stuck at the bottom.
3. Seal the lid and close the vent and set it to manual mode. Set pressure to low. The timer should be set to 35 minutes. If you want a crispy top, set the timer to 45 minutes.
4. Typically, since the pressure is low, the pot should not have sealed since there is no liquid.
5. Press the cake to test whether it has cooked. It should bounce back if well-cooked. Also, it should be pulling away from the sides.
6. Once done, use a spatula to loosen the cake from the sides. Carefully, pop it upside down. The lower part should be crispy and golden brown.
7. Serve with your favorite toppings.

Nutritional Value per serving

(excludes optionals and toppings)

- Calories: 320
- Proteins: 12g
- Fat: 3g
- Dietary Fiber: 1g
- Sugar: 10g
- Carbohydrates: 59g

Egg bites

Serving size: 12 egg bites

Estimated time: 15 minutes

Ingredients

- 8 eggs
- ¼ cup milk
- ¼ cup cheddar cheese shredded
- ½ cup diced ham/ precooked bacon
- ¼ teaspoon salt
- 1 pinch black pepper powder
- 1 green onion (optional)

Instructions

1. Spray two silicone baby food trays with non-stick cooking spray.
2. In a medium bowl, whisk together eggs, milk, green onion, salt, and pepper and ensure that they are fully blended. Divide the meat evenly in silicon cups and pour the egg mixture all over each cup. Do not fill to allow expanding space. Ideally, each cup should be filled up about two thirds.

3. Pour a cup of water in the instant pot. Place a trivet at the bottom and use a sling to lower the silicon trays. Carefully stack the trays on top of each other and lock the lid in place.
4. Select high-pressure cook and set the timer to 11 minutes. If you prefer softer eggs, set the timer to around 7-8 minutes.
5. When the cooking time ends, turn off the pressure cooker and allow a natural release. This should take about 5 minutes at most. Finish with quick pressure release and remove the lid once cooking is done.
6. Place the tray on a wire rack to allow fast cooling. Then turn the tray over and gently remove the egg bites from the trays.
7. You can add any toppings of your choice

Nutritional value per serving

(excludes optionals and toppings)

- Calories: 72
- Total fat: 5g
- Saturated fat: 2g
- Protein: 6g
- Dietary Fiber: 0g
- Sugar: 0g
- Carbohydrates: 1g

Chapter Two: Lunch Recipes

Note: Feel free to add your favorite vegetables to any of the following recipes for a well-balanced meal.

Instant Pot Barbecue Ribs

Serving Size: 2

Estimated Time: 35 min

Ingredients

- 1 rack of baby back ribs
- 1 cup of vegetable broth
- 5 tablespoons of barbecue meat rub
- 1 cup barbecue sauce
- I cup apple juice (optional)

Instructions

1. Begin by removing the membrane from the rib's back.
2. Apply meat rub generously.
3. Place the ribs in an instant pot and add vegetable broth and apple juice. Set the pot to cook on manual mode and turn off after 15-20 minutes.
4. Allow the pressure to release on its own, which may take around 5 minutes.

5. To ensure that all the pressure is gone, turn the vent to "venting" for 3 minutes, then open the lid.
6. Preheat the oven broil
7. Apply barbecue sauce all over the ribs and transfer to a large baking dish.
8. Broil for 5 minutes, until all the sauce caramelizes.
9. Remove and serve.

Nutritional value per serving

- Carbohydrates: 54g
- Protein: 42g
- Fat: 36g
- Sugar: 42g
- Saturated fat: 13g
- Dietary Fiber: 2g

Spaghetti and Meatballs

Serving size: 4

Estimated Time: 30 min

Ingredients

- 1 lb. meatballs (frozen)
- 8 oz. Spaghetti
- 24 oz. pasta sauce
- Parmesan cheese or fresh basil (optional)
- 2 cups of water
- 1 tablespoon olive oil

Instructions

1. In the instant pot, arrange the meatballs in one layer at the bottom
2. Cut the spaghetti to your desired length and place them all over the meatballs
3. Sprinkle a little olive oil on top and pour in the pasta sauce and water. Ensure that the spaghetti is fully covered.
4. Cover the instant pot, and set it to manual mode. The timer should be set at 10 minutes.
5. Once done, release the pressure and open the lid.
6. Stir in the cheese and basil.
7. Serve and enjoy

Nutritional value per serving

- Total fat: 13.6g
- Sugar: 12.1 g
- Protein: 23.1 g
- Total carbohydrates: 27.6 g
- Dietary Fiber: 0g

Chicken with Gravy

Serving size: 4

Estimated time: 25 minutes

Ingredients

- 1 cup water/chicken broth
- 6 pieces of chicken thighs (boneless and skinless)
- 1 packet onion soup mix
- 1 can of mushroom soup

Instructions

1. Put water or broth in the instant pot and add in the chicken pieces.
2. Sprinkle onion soup mix on top of the chicken. Add the mushroom soup on top, and do not stir.
3. Cover the pot and ensure that the valve is set to sealing. Set the timer to 15 minutes high-pressure, and allow to release naturally when it goes off. Once done, allow to release the rest of the pressure by moving the valve to "venting". Then, remove the lid.
4. Take out the chicken and serve.
5. Use the soup as gravy.
6. You can serve with potatoes, rice or noodles.

Nutritional value per serving

- Calories: 329
- Sugar: 0g
- Carbohydrates: 10g
- Protein: 40g
- Fat: 12g
- Fiber: 0g

Mac and Cheese

Serving size: 2

Estimated preparation time: 10 min

Ingredients

- ¼ pound whole wheat pasta uncooked
- 1 cup shredded cheese
- ¼ cup whole milk
- 3 tablespoons butter
- 4 cups of water
- Salt to taste

Instructions

1. Put water in the instant pot, add enough salt and butter, then add the whole wheat pasta.
2. Cook for 4 minutes, then remove from heat and release the steam safely.
3. The pasta should have a thin layer of buttery sauce at the top.
4. Add cheese and milk on top and gently stir.
5. Serve!

Nutritional value per serving

- Calories: 390
- Dietary Fiber: 5.2g
- Total fat: 18.2g
- Protein: 16.5g
- Sugars: 2.5g
- Carbohydrates: 43.4g

Spanish Rice

Serving size: 3

Estimated preparation time: 35 min

Ingredients

- 1 cup of brown rice
- 7 ounces diced tomatoes
- ¼ sliced yellow onion
- 1 clove minced garlic
- ½ tablespoon olive oil
- 2 cups water or vegetable broth
- Salt to taste

Instructions

1. Sauté onion, garlic, rice, and olive oil using the sauté function for 2 minutes.
2. Add the diced tomatoes, enough salt, and water/vegetable broth.
3. Stir together slowly until fully mixed.
4. Seal the instant pot and cook on high pressure for around 24 minutes.
5. Once the timer goes off, turn off the pot and allow to cool down naturally.
6. Serve!

Nutritional Value per serving

- Calories: 122 kcal
- Total fat: 1.3g
- Saturated fat: 0.11 g
- Dietary fiber: 1g
- Sugars: 3.5g
- Carbohydrates: 24g

Hawaiian Chicken

Serving size: 6

Estimated time: 15 minutes

Ingredients

- 2 pounds of chicken breasts (boneless and skinless)
- 15 oz. Hawaiian BBQ sauce
- I cup chicken broth or water
- 1 can drained sliced pineapple
- Salt and pepper to taste
- ¼ cup chopped cilantro to garnish (optional)

Instructions

1. Pour the water or chicken broth into the instant pot at the bottom.
2. Place the trivet in the pot, and place the chicken breast crossways on top. Pour ¼ of the BBQ sauce over the chicken, and make sure that it is well-spread. Sprinkle salt and pepper lightly all over the chicken.
3. Cover the instant pot and make sure that it is well secured with the lid. Set the valve to sealing to ensure that the pot is well-secured. Manually set the pressure cook to 12 minutes if it is fresh, and 15 minutes if it is frozen.

4. When the beeper goes off, allow the pot to sit for 5 minutes.
5. Move the valve to vent and remove the lid. Take out the chicken and shred on a cutting board.
6. Take out the liquid from the pot and put the shredded chicken back in.
7. Turn the settings to sauté and pour in the remaining BBQ sauce. Add in the pineapple and cilantro and stir.
8. Serve the chicken with rolls/buns or with steamed rice.
9. Enjoy!

Nutritional Value per serving

- Calories: 175
- Total fat: 0.5g
- Cholesterol: 55mg
- Total carbohydrates: 18.8g
- Sugars: 3.2g
- Fiber: 0.2g
- Sodium: 232.5mg
- Protein: 23g

Chapter Three: Dinner Recipes

Note: Feel free to add your favorite vegetables to any of the following recipes for a well-balanced meal.

Chicken Enchilada Casserole

Serving size: 2

Estimated Time: 20 min

Ingredients

- 2 chicken breasts
- 1 cup red enchilada sauce
- 2 cups grated cheddar cheese
- 10 corn tortilla stripes
- Cilantro (optional)
- Black olives (optional)
- Sour cream (optional)

Instructions

1. Put the chicken in the instant pot.
2. Pour red enchilada sauce on top.

3. Cover the pot and seal the lid. Then, set it to meat and cook for 10 minutes
4. The steam should be quickly released.
5. Once done, remove the chicken and shred using two forks. At this point, the skin is supple enough and it can easily be shredded.
6. Return to the pot, and add in half of the cheese and sliced tortillas. If you have black olives, add them in at this point.
7. Cover the pot and cook using the same meat settings for at least three minutes. This is sufficient time to melt the cheese.
8. Remove the steam naturally.
9. Serve with sour cream and sprinkle chopped cilantro on top to garnish.

Nutritional Value per serving

- Fiber: 8g
- Fat: 42g
- Sugar: 9g
- Protein: 63g

Shredded Chicken Salsa

Serving size: 4

Estimated Time: 30 min

Ingredients

- 1-pound chicken breast (skinless and boneless)
- 1 cup chunky salsa

Spices

- Enough salt and pepper to taste
- 1 pinch oregano herb powder
- ½ teaspoon cumin powder
- 1 pinch black pepper powder

Instructions

1. Season the chicken with a mixture of all the spices. Seasoning is optional, and you can use any other spices that you prefer.
2. Place the chicken in an instant pot and cover it with the chunky salsa.
3. Set the pot to 20 minutes.
4. Once done, allow the steam to naturally release.

5. Remove from pot and use a fork to shred. This part is optional, and you can cut the chicken up as you wish.

Nutritional Value per serving

- Protein: 22g
- Fiber: 1g
- Carbohydrates: 3g
- Sugar: 1g

Chicken Burrito Lasagna

Serving size: 4

Estimated time: 30 min

Ingredients

- 4 small tortillas
- 1 ½ cup salsa
- 1 cup cooked chicken
- 1 cup cheddar cheese (shredded)
- ½ can beans refried

Instructions

1. In the spring form pan of the instant pot, spray using cooking spray.
2. On a flat surface, take three tortillas and spread the refried beans over them. The spread should be even.
3. Place the first tortilla on the pan and add 1/3 of the cooked chicken.
4. Add ¼ of salsa on top of the chicken and spread evenly.
5. Sprinkle ¼ of cheese on top of the salsa.
6. Cover with a tortilla and repeat the layering. The topmost tortilla should be the one without the fried beans spread.

7. Add salsa and cheese on top of the outermost tortilla. The cheese spread should be generous.
8. Add trivet to the instant pot and put one cup of water.
9. Place the lasagna on the trivet and lock the lid. The pressure release should be turned to the back.
10. Using the manual button, set the timer to cook for 10 minutes.
11. Once done, quick-release the pressure.
12. Note that, the spring form pan is bound to be very hot at this point. Be careful when removing it.
13. Allow the lasagna to sit for at least 10 minutes before serving.
14. Enjoy!

Nutritional Value per serving

- Total fat: 32g
- Carbohydrates: 41g
- Dietary Fiber: 5g
- Sugars: 9g
- Protein: 32g

Buffalo Chicken Lettuce Wraps

Serving size: 4

Estimated time: 35 minutes

Ingredients

- 2 lb. boneless and skinless chicken thighs. The excess fat should be trimmed off.
- ½ cup buffalo sauce
- ¼ cup blue cheese crumbles
- 1 cup of water
- ½ cup chopped celery (optional)
- Washed lettuce leaves

Instructions

1. Place the chicken on top of the trivet (if frozen). If it is frozen, place the trivet at the bottom of the instant pot. If the chicken is not frozen, place the chicken at the bottom of the instant pot without a trivet.
2. Pour a cup of water at the bottom of the pot and cover the lid. Ensure that the valve is on sealing.
3. If the chicken is frozen, set the manual timer to 30 minutes on high pressure. If thawed, set the timer to 15 minutes.
4. When the beeper goes off, allow releasing naturally for 10 minutes.

5. Open the pot and drain out the water. Pour in the buffalo sauce and either shred the chicken or cut it up as you desire.
6. If you desire, stir in the chopped celery.
7. Lay lettuce leaves on a plate and place the chicken on top.
8. Top with the blue cheese crumbles
9. Enjoy!

Nutritional value per serving

- Calories: 163
- Fat: 4g
- Carbohydrates: 6g
- Dietary Fiber: 4g
- Protein: 28g
- Sugar: 0g

Mashed Ranch Cauliflower

Serving size: 5

Estimated Time: 20 minutes

Ingredients

- I head cauliflower
- 1 cup water/chicken broth
- 3 tablespoon dressing mix (dry ranch)
- 4 tablespoon butter
- 2 tablespoon milk (optional)

Instructions

1. Pour the chicken broth or water into the instant pot. Place a trivet/steam basket into the pot.
2. Remove any leaves and the core of the cauliflower. Then, put the entire head into the trivet. As an alternative, you can cut up the cauliflower into florets.
3. Cover the lid securely and make sure that the valve is set to sealing. Set the pot to manual, high-pressure cook. Set the timer to 15 minutes for the whole head. If you cut it up to florets, set the timer to 4 minutes.
4. When the timer goes off, move the valve up to venting to release pressure. Then, remove the lid.

5. Take out the cauliflower and remove the liquid. Place the cauliflower back to the pot and stir the butter and ranch dressing in. you can use a potato masher to mash the cauliflower. The level to which you mash depends on your choice of texture. If you want the cauliflower to be a little creamier, add milk and stir.
6. Serve and enjoy.

Nutritional value per serving

- Calories: 156
- Sugar: 5g
- Fat: 12g
- Carbohydrates: 12g
- Protein: 4g
- Dietary Fiber: 1g

Lime Chicken Tacos

Serving size: 4

Estimated time: 25 minutes

Ingredients

- ½ cup green taco sauce
- 2 pounds of chicken breasts (boneless and skinless)
- ½ cup chicken broth
- Avocado pieces
- 1 tablespoon grill mojito lime marinade

Instructions

1. Put ½ cup chicken broth in the instant pot.
2. Add in the chicken and pour taco sauce all over it. Add the tablespoon of mojito all over the chicken.
3. Pressure cook and begin by covering the pot and making sure that the valve settings are on sealing.
4. Set the pot to manual/pressure cook and set the timer to 12 minutes if the chicken is frozen. If fresh, set the timer to 10 minutes.
5. When the timer goes off, allow the pot to sit for 10 minutes before moving the valve to venting.

6. Remove chicken from the pot and place it on a cutting board. Shred using a fork or a knife and return it to the pot juices.
7. Stir the chicken into the juice and serve on tacos, burritos, quesadillas, and salad.
8. Add avocado slices and enjoy!

Nutritional value per serving

- Total fat: 6.2g
- Saturated fat: 2.5g
- Cholesterol: 28mg
- Potassium: 213mg
- Total carbohydrates: 19g
- Sugars: 1.3g
- Fiber: 1.2g
- Protein: 13g
- Sodium: 601mg

BONUS CHAPTER:
Chocolate Desserts

Nutella Lava Cakes

Serving size: 2

Estimated time: 25 minutes

Ingredients

- 1 whole egg and 1 yolk
- 1/3 cup Nutella
- 2 tablespoon of all-purpose flour
- 2 tablespoon of granulated white sugar (or stevia for a healthier alternative)

Instructions

1. In a small bowl, mix whole egg and egg yolk. Whisk until it becomes smooth.
2. Add in sugar and continue whisking. Then add in Nutella spread and whisk again. Finally, add in flour and whisk until any lumps disappear.
3. Grease 2 0z porcelain ramekins with cooking oil spray.
4. Divide batter among the ramekins, and ensure that you leave sufficient space for expanding.

5. Place a trivet inside the inner part of the pot. Fill with 1 cup of water.
6. Place the ramekins onto the trivet and seal the pot. Set to manual high pressure, and cook for 9 minutes.
7. When the timer goes off, do a quick release to prevent the cake from overcooking. Do not touch the ramekins with your bare hands. You can use tongs or baking gloves to remove from the heat.
8. Invert the ramekins on a plate and dust the cake with powdered sugar. The cake will be best enjoyed while warm.
9. Serve with fresh fruit.

Nutritional value per serving

- Calories: 622
- Carbohydrates: 57g
- Protein: 9g
- Fat: 40g
- Saturated fat: 29g
- Dietary Fiber: 2g
- Suga

Chocolate Pots De Crème

Serving size: 6

Estimated time: 30 minutes

Ingredients

- 2 cups of heavy cream
- ½ cup whole milk
- 5 large egg yolks
- 8-ounce bittersweet melted chocolate (low in sugar)
- ¼ cup of sugar (or stevia for a healthier alternative)
- Salt to taste
- Grated chocolate for decoration

Instructions

1. In a small saucepan, bring milk and cream to a simmer.
2. In a large bowl, whisk together sugar, salt, and egg yolks. Add in melted chocolate and continue whisking until they are fully blended.
3. Pour mixture into custard cups.
4. Put 2 cups of water into an instant pot and place a trivet at the bottom. Place three custard cups on the trivet and place the second trivet on top of the cups. Stack any remaining custard cups therein.

5. Lock the lid in place and select high pressure. Put the timer to 6 minutes. When it beeps, turn off the pressure cooker and release it naturally for 15 minutes. Afterward, do a quick release to remove any remaining pressure.
6. Once the timer goes off, carefully remove the lid.
7. Remove the pots de crème and leave to cool.
8. Serve.

Nutritional value per serving

- Fat: 39g
- Cholesterol: 124g
- Sugars: 20g
- Protein: 4g

Conclusion

Thank you again for purchasing this book!

I hope this book provided you with a good introduction to the benefits of the Instant Pot and how it can save you on time, money and ultimately your health! And for those that have more experience using an instant pot, I hope this provided you with a few new, simple and tasty recipes for you to try and add into your busy lifestyle.

Please leave a review!

A lot of research and work goes into our books to make the content the best quality for you – our customers. Therefore, we would love it if you left us a review on Amazon! Please go to:

http://www.amazon.com/review/create-review?&asin=B087QR2Z9H

Any comments would be greatly appreciated. We take all comments very seriously and use these comments to update the content and quality of our books for.

Made in the USA
Columbia, SC
26 May 2020